IMPACT!

THE LEGACY OF THE WOMEN'S CAUCUS FOR ART

Curated by Leslie King-Hammond

IMPACT!
The Legacy of the Women's Caucus for Art

Curated by: Leslie King-Hammond
Co-Organized by Barbara Wolanin and Jaimianne Amicucci
Cover by: Amanda Moyer
Timeline by: Barbara Wolanin

ISBN-13: 978-1523808106

Women's Caucus for Art
www.nationalwca.org

The mission of the Women's Caucus for Art is to create community through art, education, and social activism. WCA is committed to recognizing the contribution of women in the arts; providing women with leadership opportunities and professional development; expanding networking and exhibition opportunities for women; supporting local, national and global art activism; and advocating for equity in the arts for all.

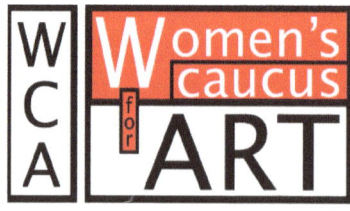

AMERICAN UNIVERSITY MUSEUM
at the Katzen Center

TABLE OF CONTENTS

LENDERS

American University Museum, Washington, DC
Helène Aylon
Judith K. Brodsky
Diane Burko
DC Moore Gallery, New York, NY
Goya Contemporary, Baltimore, MD
Jack Rutberg Fine Arts , Los Angeles, CA
James E. Lewis Museum, Morgan State University, Baltimore, MD
Michael Rosenfeld Gallery LLC, New York, NY
National Museum of Women in the Arts, Washington, DC
Private Collections
Reginald F. Lewis Museum, Baltimore, MD
Joyce J. Scott
Dr. Diane Whitfield Locke and John Woo

Publications lent by HIRO, Helen Langa,
Leslie King-Hammond, Barbara Wolanin

1969

Women Artists in Revolution (WAR) launched protests against museums and galleries exhibiting few women artists.

1970

Women's Art Registry created to gather information about women artists and is still maintained at Rutgers University.

The Women's Interart Center was founded in New York City.

Judy Chicago taught separate women's studio art classes at Fresno State, CA.

Women in the Arts founded in New York City.

1971

Judy Chicago and Miriam Schapiro initiate The Feminist Art Program at the California Institute of the Arts; its Womanhouse project brought feminist art to national prominence.

FOREWORD

BY JACK RASMUSSEN

It is appropriate that *IMPACT! Legacy of the Women's Caucus for Art* should be exhibited in the American University Museum at the Katzen Arts Center. American University's Art History program was led for many years by Mary Garrard and Norma Broude, two major pioneers of Feminist Art History, who were, respectively, the second president and first affirmative action officer of Women's Caucus for Art in the mid-1970s. The exhibition they curated here in 2006, *Claiming Space: Some American Feminist Originators*, established the museum as an important venue for powerful ideas and provocative art. The University's strength in this arena grew as the current faculty were added, including Helen Langa, Kim Butler, Juliet Bellow, Andrea Pearson, and Ying-chen Peng, all of whom take feminist art history as a significant aspect of their research and teaching.

Many more people were involved in *IMPACT!* than I can thank by name here, but two participants must be singled out. Curator Leslie King-Hammond took on the formidable task of researching and looking at all the distinguished artists who received WCA's Lifetime Achievement Award over the past forty-four years and created an exhibition that is a testimony to the efforts of all the artists who have supported this important and necessary organization. Barbara Wolanin, who retired as Curator for the Architect of the Capitol only to work more than full time for the past year herding cats, boxing frogs, pulling teeth, and anything else necessary to bring this exhibition to

1972

Linda Nochlin's classic article, "Why Have There Been No Great Women Artists?" was published in ArtNews.

"Where We At" Black Women Artists (WWA) cooperative was formed following their exhibition in New York City.

The Women's Caucus for Art was conceived in a meeting of artists and art historians during the January 1972 College Art Association meeting in San Francisco.

Founding of *Heresies: A Feminist Publication on Art and Politics*, which was published from 1977 to 1992 by the Heresies Collective in New York, which included Harmony Hammond, Lucy R. Lippard, Miriam Schapiro, May Stevens and others.

you. Our appreciation also must be expressed to Jaimianne Amicucci, the Women's Caucus for the Art Board of Directors, WCA President Brenda Oelbaum, Marilyn Hayes, Giselle Huberman, Kristi-Anne Caisse, and all of our wonderful, talented, and dedicated staff.

Jack Rasmussen
Director and Curator
American University Museum
Katzen Arts Center

1973

The Feminist Art Journal (1972-77) was founded, with Cindy Nemser as editor-in-chief.

The first national conference on women in the visual arts was held at the California Institute of the Arts and the Corcoran School of Art in Washington, DC

The not-for-profit A.I.R. Gallery in New York was created to exhibit the work of women artists. The twenty co-founders included Nancy Spero, Harmony Hammond, and Howardena Pindell.

The Feminist Studio Workshop was founded in Los Angeles by Judy Chicago, Arlene Raven, and Sheila Levrant de Bretteville. Participants created the Woman's Building to show women's art.

The collective gallery Artemisia opened in Chicago and the Women's Art Registry of Minnesota started WARM Gallery.

ACKNOWLEDGMENTS

BY BRENDA OELBAUM

We are very appreciative of American University and Director Jack Rasmussen's enthusiasm about collaborating on an exhibition to honor the legacy of the Women's Caucus for Art (WCA) with an exhibition of the Lifetime Achievement Awardees, a tribute that has been honoring outstanding women in the visual arts since 1979. It is very fitting that the exhibition be at American University, known for its commitment to feminist art history and its long connection to WCA.

Not long after becoming President Elect of the National Women's Caucus for Art, it was announced that the College Art Association would be holding their 2016 conference in Washington, DC, for the first time in over two decades. The significance of a DC conference, the city where the WCA held its first awards in 1979, was not lost on either WCA member and historian, Barbara Wolanin or myself. We immediately started to discuss ideas for the WCA conference and possible exhibitions, themes, and venues. I had always hoped that WCA would mount an exhibition that would focus on its Lifetime Achievement Awardees and it was wonderful to learn Barbara had the same idea in mind. Washington, DC would be the perfect location, based on WCA's history, DC's proximity to museums and collections that contained works by many of our honorees. With esteemed curator and past Lifetime Achievement Award honoree, Leslie King-Hammond, just over the state line in Baltimore, we believed this idea could get off

1974

Chicano Las Mujeres Muralistas formed.

The second WCA president, art historian Mary Garrard (1974-76), assisted by Secretary Ellouise Schoettler, Affirmative Action Officer Norma Broude, and other members of Washington Women Art Professionals, incorporated the WCA with non-profit status, created a national network of local chapters, and convinced CAA to give WCA official status as an affiliated society meeting with the annual CAA conference.

1975

WCA was an official presence at the CAA conference in Washington, DC, holding three workshops on the problems of women artists, art historians and museum professionals. More WCA panels and program events were held at CAA's Chicago conference in 1976.

the ground in a dramatic and positive way. Barbara engaged Jaimianne Amicucci of WCA Young Women's Caucus to partner with her, and they prepared a detailed proposal for the approval of the WCA board. Organizing and developing the exhibition has been an enormous job and much harder to accomplish than anyone involved had imagined but if this idea was to become a reality, this was indeed the time.

IMPACT! The Legacy of the Women's Caucus of Art stands to show that after almost half a century, acknowledging women in the arts is still important. The Women's Caucus for Art continues this tradition by annually honoring women who show excellence in the arts. With this exhibition, we strengthen the history and future of the organization, the Lifetime Achievement Awards and set a precedent for future WCA museum exhibitions.

I want to acknowledge and thank the many people who made this exhibition possible. Thank you to Leslie King-Hammond for her ideas and enthusiasm and her personal connections with artists, galleries, and institutions that made the exhibition possible. Director and Curator Jack Rasmussen and Assistant Director Kristi-Anne Caisse, for their faith in and substantial support in this project, and to their skilled staff as well as to American University. Great thanks to all of the lenders for their critical support. Thanks to Professors Helen Langa and Mary Garrard for their support and to the AU students who worked on artist biographies.

Finally, I appreciate Jaimianne Amicucci and Amanda Rogers for their work on the exhibition and the catalog, Marilyn Hayes for her financial and emotional support, Giselle Huberman for her

1976   1977

Spiderwoman Theater was founded by Muriel Miguel and her sisters Gloria Miguel and Lisa Mayo.

WCA held its first national conference and first national exhibition in Los Angeles in conjunction with the CAA conference. Linda Nochlin and Ann Sutherland Harris's groundbreaking exhibition *Women Artists: 1550 to 1950* was on view at the Los Angeles County Museum of Art, later traveling to Brooklyn, Pittsburgh, and Austin TX.

Under third president Judith K. Brodsky (1976-78), WCA joined with 75 other arts organizations in the Coalition of Women's Art Organizations (CWAO) to lobby Congress and organize political actions. WCA published course syllabi compiled by Athena Tacha in Women's Studies in the Arts, while Eleanor Dickinson began an ongoing effort to gather and publish statistics documenting discrimination in the art world.

generous contribution, and finally, Barbara Wolanin, for none of this would be possible without her many hours of time volunteered, unequaled determination, vision, and leadership skills.

Brenda Oelbaum
National President
Women's Caucus for Art

The New York Feminist Art Institute was founded by Nancy Azara, Miriam Schapiro, and others.

Judy Chicago's *Dinner Party* was exhibited at the San Francisco Museum of Modern Art and toured internationally for nine years.

The first Honor Awards for Lifetime Achievement in the Visual Arts were presented by President and Mrs. Jimmy Carter at the White House to Georgia O'Keeffe (in absentia), Louise Nevelson, Alice Neel, Selma Burke, and Isabel Bishop, followed by a repeat ceremony for WCA members at the conference in Washington, DC, with their achievement documented in a catalogue. Galleries, colleges, and universities exhibited work by women during the conference.

INTRODUCTION

BY BARBARA WOLANIN AND JAIMIANNE AMICUCCI

IMPACT! The Legacy of the Women's Caucus for Art highlights the historical importance of the Women's Caucus for Art (WCA) and its success in recognizing the achievements of women in the visual arts. This exhibition includes a small selection of art and of publications by Lifetime Achievement awardees borrowed from area museums, galleries, and collectors, and celebrates all of the awardees who have been honored since the first awards were presented at the White House in 1979.

Founded in 1972, WCA is an affiliated society of the College Art Association. In 2016, both organizations held their national conferences in Washington, DC WCA is a national feminist networking organization for women in the visual arts with members in chapters across the country. The organization is unique in its multidisciplinary, multicultural membership of artists, art historians, students, educators, and museum professionals. WCA is an NGO of the United Nations and a founding member of The Feminist Art Project. WCA is committed to recognizing the contribution of women in the arts; providing women with leadership opportunities and professional development; expanding networking and exhibition opportunities for women; supporting local, national and global art activism; and advocating for equity in the arts for all.

1980

The CAA conference was held in New Orleans, LA, in a state that had not ratified the Equal Rights Amendment. WCA members who attended vowed to spend no money in the state. An alternative, protest conference was held in Washington, DC by WCA and CWAO called "Social Change Takes Courage," where awards were presented to prominent feminist activists.

The *Woman's Art Journal*, founded and edited by Elsa Honig Fine, was first published; it continues today, edited by Joan Marter and Peggy Barlow.

1983

WCA grows with chapters across the country. Sixth president, Muriel Magenta (1982-84) established a permanent national office at the Moore College of Art in Philadelphia, whose administrator created an expanded newsletter, a membership directory, and a website with work of women artists.

The WCA mission is to create community through art, education, and social activism and it has carried out its mission to recognize and document women in the visual arts through its annual Lifetime Achievement Awards. The 36th awards ceremony in 2016 brings the number of women artists, art historians, curators, and activists honored to 194.

This exhibition is a celebration of the awards program and all the women who have been honored between 1979 and 2016. The exhibition shows the impact women have had on one another by working together for a cause. The national WCA conference and its awards ceremony have been held in Washington, DC two times previous, in 1979 and 1991. In 1980 awards were also presented at an alternative WCA conference when the official conference was in New Orleans and Louisiana had not passed the ERA.

When WCA began, not one female artist was included in art history survey textbooks, most college professors with tenure were male, few works by women artists were exhibited in museums, and very few women were in leadership positions. Opportunities for women in the arts, and awareness of their contributions have improved significantly because of the efforts of WCA and other feminist organizations through the activism and the dedicated work of strong individuals. These individuals include the WCA founders, leaders, and Lifetime Achievement Award honorees, as can be seen in the milestones summarized across the introductory pages to provide a context for the exhibition.

Today women are still under-represented in museums, galleries, and publications,

1985

President Annie Shaver-Crandall (1986-1988) oversaw the establishment of the WCA archives at Rutgers University.

The Guerrilla Girls, *Conscience of the Art World,* was formed by seven women artists whose anonymous response to a Museum of Modern Art exhibition led to an ongoing campaign to bring attention to unequal treatment of women artists, through posters, publications, and public appearances in gorilla masks.

1987

The national WCA conference was organized by artists, curators, and art historians in the Boston chapter, who got over 60 academic and commercial galleries to show work by women artists.

1991

The Jewish Women Artists Network (JWAN) was formed as the first WCA special interest group. Some student chapters were formed.

and the work continues with the new generation of feminists. The CAA board has had many women presidents, including Leslie King-Hammond, the curator of this exhibition. Despite all of the gains, many of the women who teach in colleges are adjuncts, women artists are underrepresented in galleries and museums, and the world is filled with threats to women and to our natural resources. These are all issues that concern current WCA members, and the work continues with the new generation of young women. This exhibition is a result of our efforts to remedy the divide.

Barbara Wolanin, Past Women's Caucus for Art Board Member
Jaimianne Amicucci, Past Young Women's Caucus Chair
Co-Organizers of the Impact! The Legacy of the Women's Caucus for Art

1992

1994

1995

President Jean Towgood (1992-1994) created a Vice President of Women of Color and the curated the *Women of Color in the Arts* slide series that was made available to teachers.

The Power of Feminist Art: The American Movement of the 1970s, History and Impact, edited by Norma Broude and Mary D. Garrard, was published (New York: Harry N. Abrams), as the first comprehensive book on the feminist art movement in the U.S.

One hundred WCA members participated in the 1995 International Conference on Women and NGO Forum of the United Nations in China. The WCA remains a United Nations NGO and members participate in international exchanges.

12

IMPACT!

BY LESLIE KING-HAMMOND

In the past forty-four years, the Women's Caucus for Art (WCA), founded in 1972, has witnessed a prolific increase in the aesthetic innovations, artistic production, and critical scholarship by women artists, critics, curators, historians, scholars, thought leaders and activists. These highly accomplished women are formidable, tenacious, determined, and gifted with an abundance of passion, vision, technical facility, and intellectual genius. The brilliance of their creative energies is too often erased from the discourse before the discourse of the day has begun. The reality is that female artists have exacted on the landscape of the mainstream art world profound impressions, interpretations, and images of the world they experience from a very intimate and personal point of view. The IMPACT of these female makers and artistic intellectuals is a serious force of nature that must be reconciled within a more thorough and thoughtful discourse that positions the authenticity and agency of the female voice into the inner sanctum of the established white male-centric canons of the mainstream art world. The role of women in the arts demands greater contextualization within all the genres of the arts. *IMPACT!* highlights a selection of women, out of over 194 individuals, who have been honored by the Women's Caucus for Art with a Lifetime Achievement Award. This exhibition represents a very small fraction of the remarkable achievements and brilliant creativity of not just the awardees but also the entire WCA membership and non-members, to whom this organization works to advocate for opportunity and inclusion in all aspects of the art world.

1997-1998

Factors including holding the WCA conference in Philadelphia separate from the CAA conference in New York and the move of the national office to New York City, brought WCA close to bankruptcy. The efforts of the membership and the transitional leadership committee with an auction of donated art organized by Gail Tremblay, ensured WCA's survival and return to financial stability.

1999

Under president Magi Amma (2000-2002), the member database, newsletter, website, and national awards were revived and the national board instituted a reserve fund.

The Los Angeles' chapter led a successful conference and an awards ceremony during the CAA conference, co-organized by Ada Brown and Jean Towgood.

Traditional histories tend to validate women artists by comparing them to a male mentor figure or as Joyce Kozloff has observed after viewing many exhibitions of woman artists, "… the accompanying texts place them in an artistic context comprised solely of their husbands, boyfriends and guy colleagues – as if their acclaim had separated them from their female peers." (1) The real story to be researched and critiqued is about how women influenced, inspired, challenged, supported, and provided an invaluable infrastructure crucial to each other's aesthetic and intellectual development. Through partnerships, alliances, unions, collaborations, friendships, affiliations, and kinships, women worked with each other to critically shape their development as artists, critics, scholars, and thought leaders. Women became agents of aesthetic change, who defined and executed remarkably innovative strategies that created unique teaching models, workshops, studio spaces, project and performance events, and initiatives that explored alternative possibilities of creativity and artistry. *IMPACT!* is a celebration of not just the survival of women in the visual arts. It is an act of peer recognition that affirms the role of the WCA within the canon of the legacy of the visual arts traditions in the United States.

Too often the importance and status of award recognition is biased towards long-standing, established organizations. The WCA was an inspiration that came into being after starting out as a sub-committee of the College Art Association (CAA). In the history of the CAA, founded in 1911, there have been twelve elected female presidents out of forty-one elections. Four of the CAA presidents–Marilyn Skokstad, Ruth Weisberg, Judy Brodsky, and Leslie King-Hammond–are also WCA awardees who worked to keep an active female presence on the agenda of the CAA's national programming. The actions of the CAA and the WCA brought increased awareness and

2002

2006

President Noreen Dean Dresser (2004-2006) hired Karin Luner as the national administrator, which made membership rebound.

President Dena Muller arranged for a small national office at Rutgers University.

The WCA Boston chapter organized an in-depth conference which demonstrated how meaningful the WCA has been to members. The papers and other essays, edited by Karen Frostig and Kathy A. Halamka, were published in *Blaze: Discourse on Art, Women and Feminism* in 2007.

WCA became a founding partner of The Feminist Art Project (TFAP), organized at Rutgers University, which documents and celebrates the feminist art movement.

attention to the art world's exclusion of women. For women outside the participation and affiliation of these two organizations, these concerns have also always been points of contest, for all women throughout history. By the time Betty Friedan published *The Feminine Mystique* in 1963 the seeds of social and political dissent were already sown and Friedan's book became a catalyst for change that helped to fuel and define the beginnings of the Feminist Movement.

In 1971, with the publication of WCA awardee Linda Nochlin's seminal essay, "Why Have There Been No Great Women Artists," The Feminist Movement was officially launched in the psyche and passions of women seeking parity in all aspects of the arts. The *IMPACT!* exhibition is an opportunity to reflect upon the artistic work, as well as the many roles women played during the WCA's mission to support the vision, production, and intellect of women artists. Collaboration was one of the most successful and easily accessed strategies that allowed women to organize more effectively to focus on specific projects. Judy Chicago and Miriam Schapiro conceived and collaborated with numerous women to create an iconic work of monumental importance in Womanhouse (1972). In the absence of adequate studio space, an old deserted mansion in a residential community in Hollywood, California, became an installation and performance space that focused on meanings and experiences specific to the lives of woman. The African-American communities in Los Angeles benefited greatly from the tireless efforts of artists-scholars Ruth Waddy and Samella Lewis, who published surveys and organized numerous exhibitions for disenfranchised artists of African descent during the era of the Black Arts Movement (1965-1975). Evangeline Montgomery, designer and printmaker who also worked with of Waddy and Lewis, went on to work for the SITES program at the Smithsonian where she was able to assist

2007

How American Women Artists Invented Postmodernism, 1970-1975, curated by Judith K. Brodsky and Ferris Olin, at Rutgers University, was the opening exhibition of TFAP.

Major feminist art exhibitions were held in the U.S., including: *WACK!: Women Artists and the Feminist Revolution* (Museum of Contemporary Art, LA and National Museum of Women in the Arts, DC), *Global Feminisms: New Directions in Contemporary Art* (Brooklyn Museum of Art, NY), and *Claiming Space: Some American Feminist* Originators (American University Museum, DC).

WCA collaborated with the CAA Committee on Women in the Arts on the joint awards ceremony in New York.

many artists of color and women in the 1980's and 1990's.

Grace Hartigan and Joan Mitchell, colleagues and friends, are recognized as significant members of the Second Generation of the Abstractionist Expressionists (1950-1960s). While neither artist felt particularly endeared to Feminist ideologies, they were in fact both pivotal models of tenacity, artistic excellence, and anti-racism who generously provided financial and intellectual support to younger artists. In founding of the Joan Mitchell Foundation (1993), it was Grace Hartigan, then director of the Hoffberger School of Painting at the Maryland Institute College of Art, who provided counsel on how to structure programmatic support for young emerging artists and recent MFA graduates. The recognition and visibility of Hartigan and Mitchell can be contrasted with the emergence and anonymity of the Guerrilla Girls, who appeared in 1985 in New York City wearing gorilla masks to hide their identity. It will probably never be known how many of the WCA awardees were active members or participants of Guerilla Girls, but it is not unreasonable to assume that there were many since there is a commonality of concern for the same issues. This group is actively devoted to fighting racism and sexism, especially in public space with posters and handouts. Grace Hartigan was often delighted with the IMPACT of the performance and politics of their protests.

The power of kinships, partnerships, and commitments to cultural heritage and family can never be underestimated or dismissed, especially where women are concerned. Women are the keepers, protectors, healers and seers of the family, community, and ancestral traditions. Betye Saar, master of mixed media and found objects, is the matriarch of a dynasty of art makers that is the legacy of

2009

Judy Chicago's *Dinner Party* found a permanent home at the Elizabeth A. Sackler Center for Feminist Art at the Brooklyn Museum of Art.

College art students, chaired by Yueh-mei Cheng, formed the Young Women's Caucus (YoungWC) to help women under 39 network and mentor new leaders.

CAA presented the first Distinguished Feminist Award to the Guerilla Girls. This award replaced the Annual Recognition Awards given by CAA's Committee on Women in the Arts from 1996 to 2008.

Under the leadership of Marilyn Hayes and Janice Nesser-Chu, the mission statement was revised to focus more on activism. Summer regional conferences were organized to coincide with the summer board meeting.

her family. Her achievement as a WCA awardee is only second to the fact that she has mentored two daughters, Alison and Lesley Saar, who have become commanding artists in their own rights. Similarly, fiber artist Elizabeth Talford Scott was a profound influence on her daughter, multimedia-performance artist, Joyce Jane Scott. Arlene Raven and Nancy Grossman, art critic and sculptor, formed a lifelong partnership and worked with countless young artists and students. The power of love, the respect for life, and the integrity and belief in the strength of these relations begs for serious scholarship to address the dynamic IMPACT that these relationships have had on the development of each of these individual artistic legacies.

The remarkable contributions of the WCA, or the Feminist movement would not have been possible without the bold and fearless scholarship of gifted scholars and historians, to many to mention for this brief overview. However, in keeping with the primary focus of this review it is the work of art historians like Norma Broude and Mary Garrard who have co-authored numerous publications on Feminist art and art history that helped to define and preserve the earliest phases of this movement. In the curatorial alliances of Lowery S. Sims, Tritobia Benjamin and myself, numerous projects and publications allowed these scholars, working like training partners, challenging each other to retrieve, define, identify and preserve lost histories and lives of artist of color and women who have suffered exclusion through benign neglect, selective amnesia, or blatant discrimination. The scholarship and artistry of Jane-Quick-to-See Smith, Amalia Mesa-Baines and Margo Machida bring balance, order, and reality to the dynamic vibrancy and resilience of the American experience. The critical and demanding role of the WCA, its stellar roster of distinguished awardees, and the entire WCA membership will continue to

2010

The first feminist art history conference, *Continuing the Legacy: Honoring the Work of Norma Broude and Mary Garrard* took place at American University, DC.

The WCA Eco-Arts Caucus grew out of the regional "Elements" Conference in Berkeley, CA. The New Media Caucus formed following years of presenting Femlink juried video shorts.

2011

Janice Nesser-Chu launched a legacy campaign with a generous bequest from Sylvia Sleigh.

!Women Art Revolution, a documentary about feminist art history debuts.

WCA exhibition *Reversing the Gaze: Man as Object*, organized by Brenda Oelbaum, Priscilla Otani, Karen Gutfreund, and Tanya Augsburg seen at SOMArts Cultural Center, San Francisco, CA and traveled to University of Indiana, Bloomington, IN

create IMPACT with relentless determination. It is now time for the currents of history to record, affirm, and acknowledge these contributions that are fundamental to our understanding of American heritage as imagined and expressed by all of its citizens.

Leslie King-Hammond
Curator, *IMPACT! The Legacy of the Women's Caucus of Art*

1.) Joyce Kozloff, "Maria Lassnig in New York, 1968-1980" Hyperallergic, November 8, 2014, http://hyperallergic.com/159289/maria-lassnig-in-new-york-1968-1980/

2012		**2014**	**2015**	**2016**
The WCA International Committee is converted to a caucus.	WCA celebrated its 40th anniversary in Los Angeles with a special awards catalog.	WCA International Caucus organized *Half the Sky: Interventions in Social Practice Art* Cultural Exchange and Exhibition in Shenyang, China.	WCA exhibition curated by Karen Gutfreund. *Views from the Edge: Women, Gender and Politics* at Brown University, Providence, RI, wins curator award for Women's History Month.	The WCA national conference is held in Washington, DC for the first time in 25 years, with an exhibition honoring women honored with Lifetime Achievement Awards.

WORKS IN THE EXHIBITION

IMPACT! The Legacy of the Women's Caucus for Art highlights the historical importance of the of the Women's Caucus for Art (WCA) and its success in recognizing the achievements of women in the visual arts. This exhibition includes only a small selection of art and of publications by Lifetime Achievement Award honorees borrowed from area museums, galleries, and collectors. It celebrates all of the awardees who have been honored since the first awards were presented at the White House in 1979.

Founded in 1972, WCA is a national feminist networking organization for women in the visual arts with members in chapters across the country and an affiliated society of the College Art Association. WCA advocates equity in the arts for all and is unique in its multidisciplinary, multicultural membership of artists, art historians, students, educators, and museum professionals. Its mission is to create community through art, education, and social activism.

WCA carries out its mission to recognize and document women in the visual arts through its annual Lifetime Achievement Awards. The 36th awards ceremony in 2016 brings the number of women artists, art historians, curators, and activists honored to 194.

HELÈNE AYLON

Helène Aylon (b. 1931) is an artist whose 50 years of multimedia work moved from process art, anti-nuclear art, and eco-feminism, to The G-d Project, a feminist commentary on the Hebrew Bible and traditions. Her focus is on rescuing the Body, Earth, G-d, Foremothers, and Civilization from patriarchal designations.

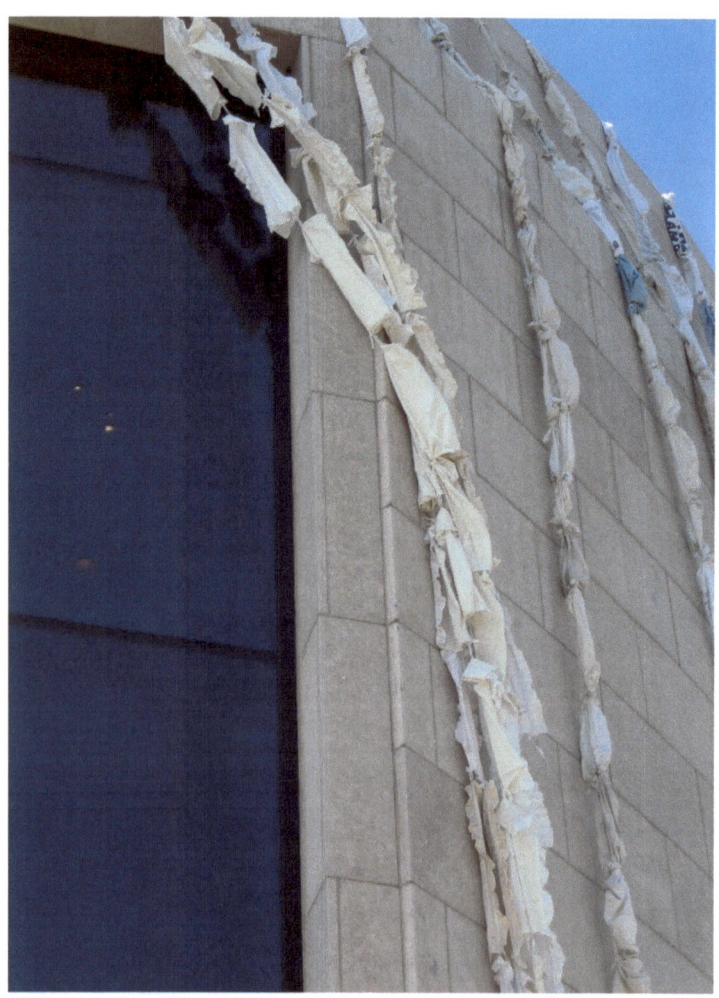

HELÈNE AYLON Awarded 2016
Bridge of Knots II, 2006
Video, 6 min 17 seconds,
Video documentation of the 2006 American University Museum
facade installation with audio by Meredith Monk
Courtesy of the Artist

ISABEL BISHOP

Isabel Bishop (1902-1988) was a painter and graphic artist who depicted the urban life and people of New York City. She is known for her images of women and people she observed in the city streets. She was a leading member of the 14th Street School.

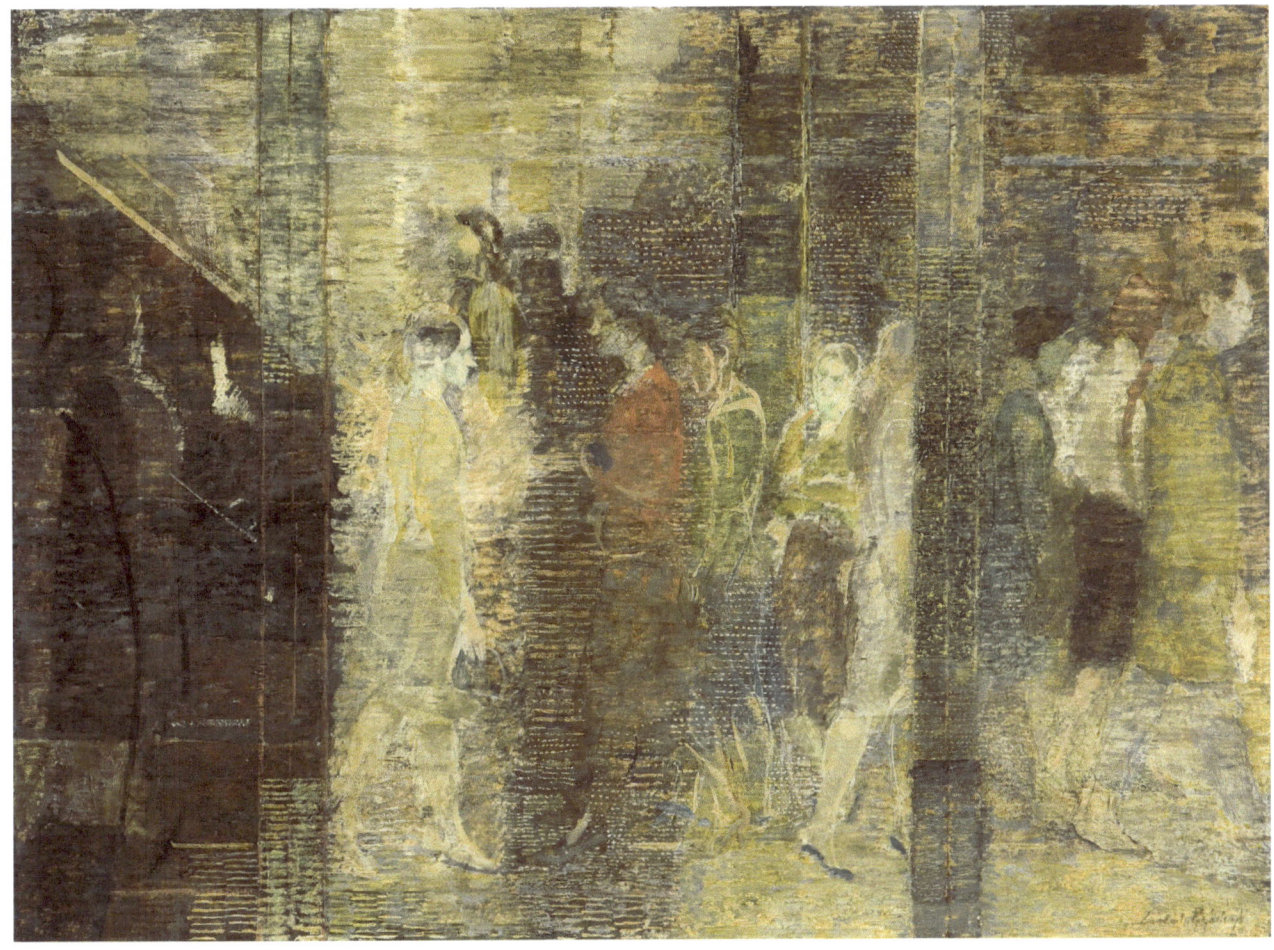

ISABEL BISHOP Awarded in 1979
Walking in the Subway Station, 1963
Oil on board, 24 x 33 in.
Courtesy of Michael Rosenfeld Gallery LLC, New York NY

JUDITH BRODSKY

Judith K. Brodsky (b. 1933) is an artist, printmaker, educator, and feminist leader. Her art explores feminism, ageism, the environment, and family. She was the third president of WCA and is a former president of CAA. She founded the Rutgers Center for Innovative Print and Paper in 1986 (now the Brodsky Center). Since the award, she co-founded and co-directs the Rutgers Institute for Women and Arts which oversees The Feminist Art Project.

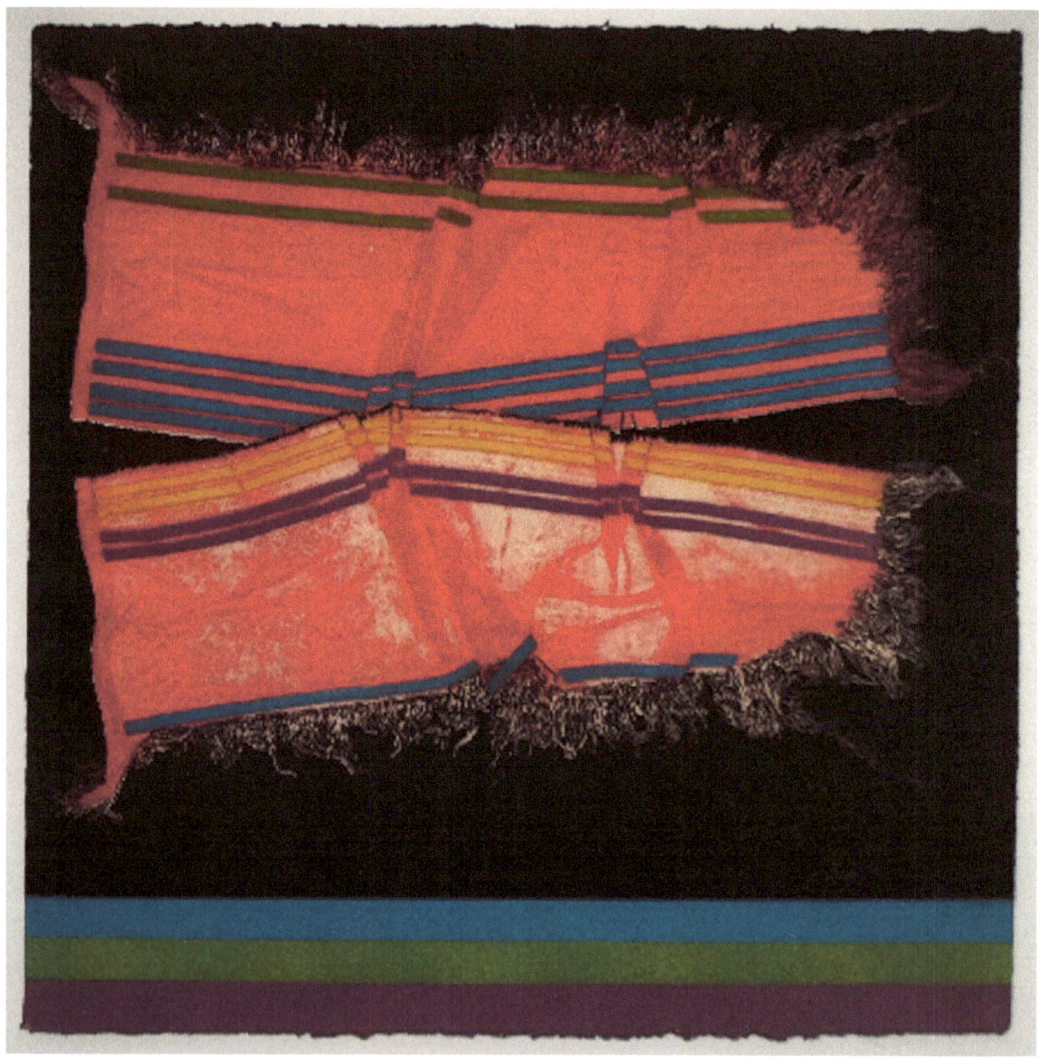

JUDITH BRODSKY   Awarded in 2002
Dishrag Diagrammatic, 1978
Intaglio and relief, 20 x 20 in.
Published by Queenston Press for first UN Year of the Woman
Courtesy of Judith K. Brodsky

BEVERLY BUCHANAN

Beverly Buchanan (1940-2015) was a highly respected artist and social commentator. Her sculptures and drawings focused on the vernacular architecture of African-American communities, from former slave houses to sharecropper shacks, suggesting the courage, strength, and resilience of their inhabitants.

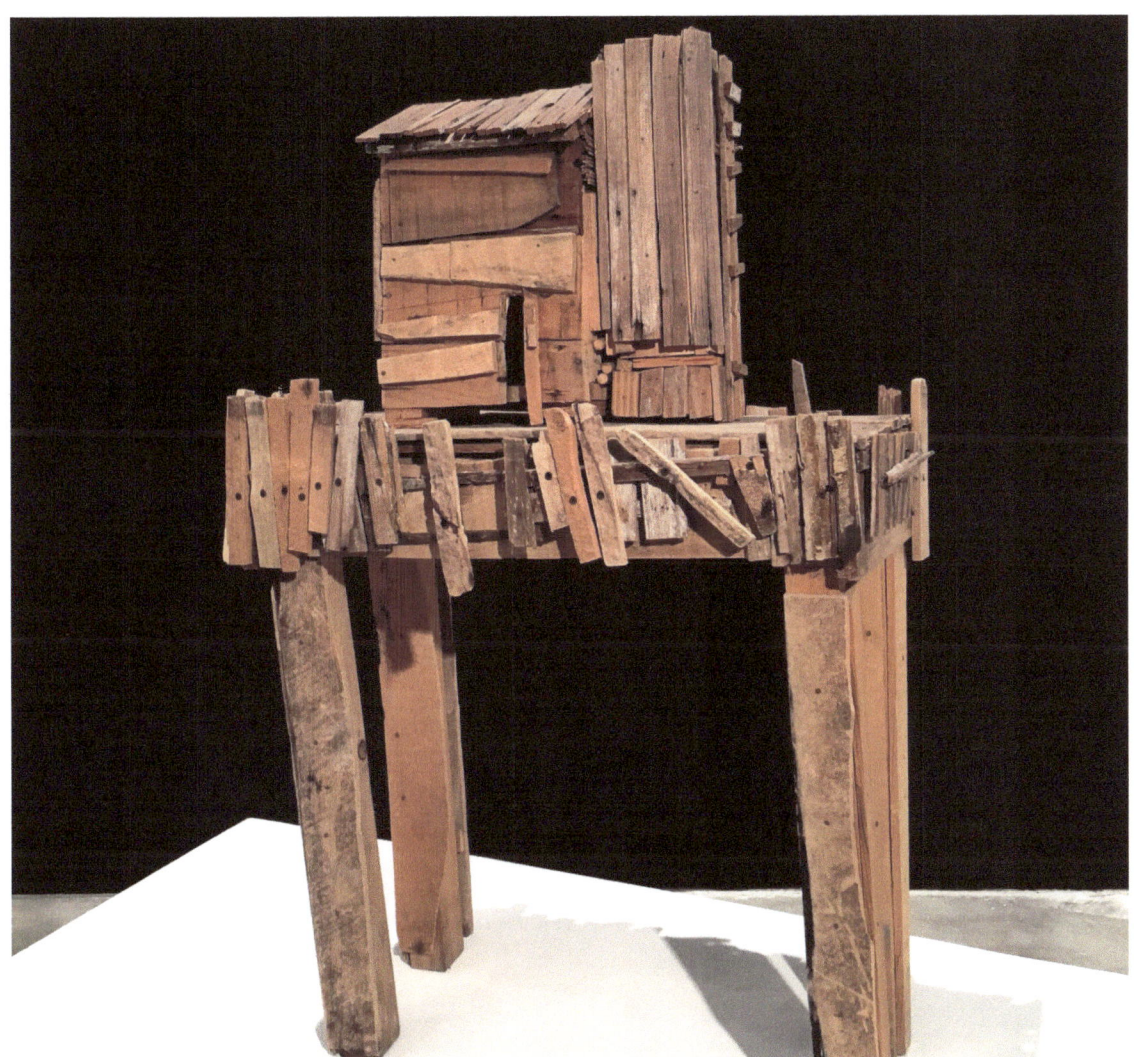

BEVERLY BUCHANAN   Awarded in 2011
Shack, 1988
Wood and nails, 43 x 30 x 17 in. (house)
33 x 31 x 17 in. (table support)
Courtesy of Reginald F. Lewis Museum

SELMA BURKE

Selma Burke (1900-1995) was a sculptor and educator known for her expressive portraits and figures. She was part of the Harlem Renaissance. Her relief portrait of President Roosevelt inspired the design of the dime. She founded two art schools, one in New York City and the Selma Burke Art Center in Pittsburgh (1968-1982).

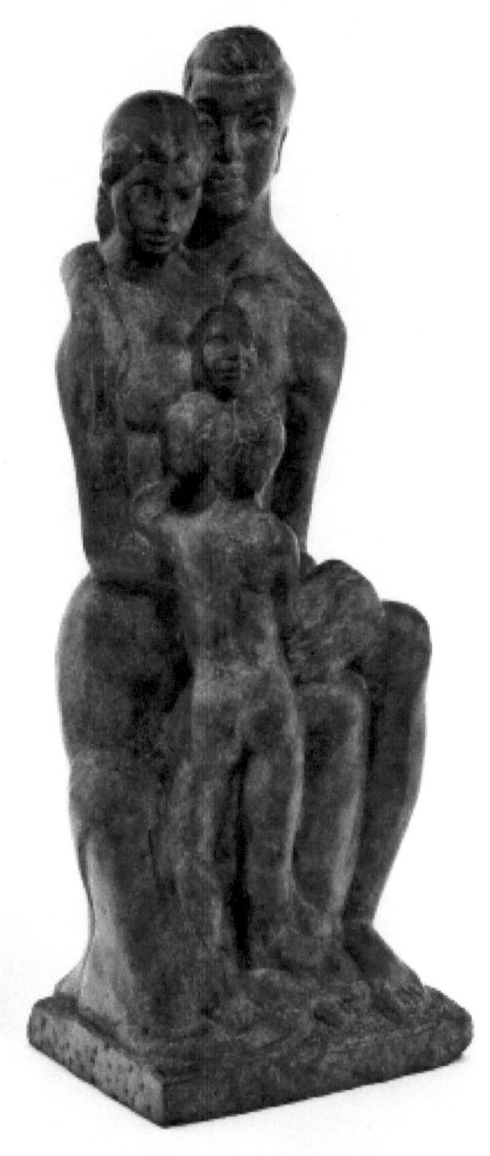

SELMA BURKE   Awarded in 1979
Family, c. 1950
Bronze, 42.375 x 14 x 15.25 in.
Courtesy of Michael Rosenfeld Gallery LLC,
New York NY

DIANE BURKO

Diane Burko (b. 1945) is a landscape painter, photographer, dedicated educator, and a pioneer of feminist art who was a founding member and director of the Women's Caucus for Art. She is a witness of climate change through her panoramic landscapes documenting melting glaciers.

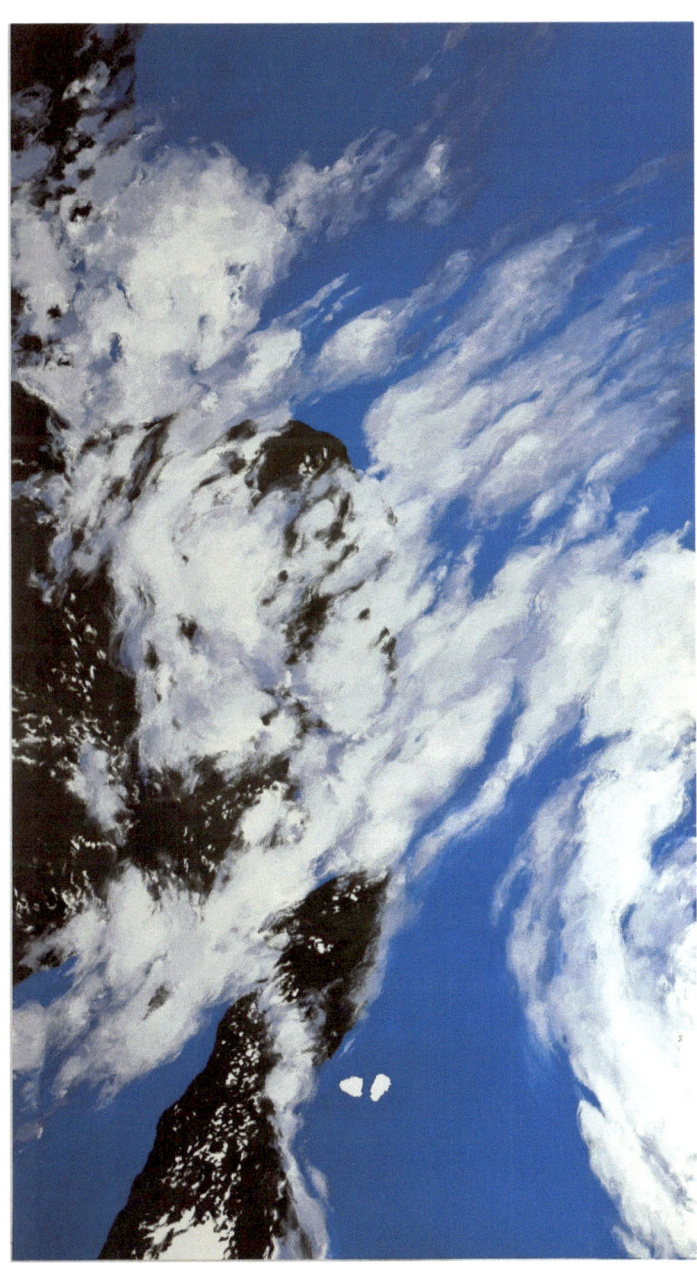

DIANE BURKO   Awarded in 2011
Peterman Heading South (after NASA), 2010-2011, 2012
Oil on canvas, 88 x 50 in.
Courtesy of the Artist

MARGARET BURROUGHS

Margaret Taylor Burroughs (1915-2010) was a painter, printmaker, writer, curator, educator, and collector. She was a scholar of African-American and African culture. She was the principal founder of the Du Sable Museum of African-American History in Chicago. She also helped found The National Council of Negro Artists.

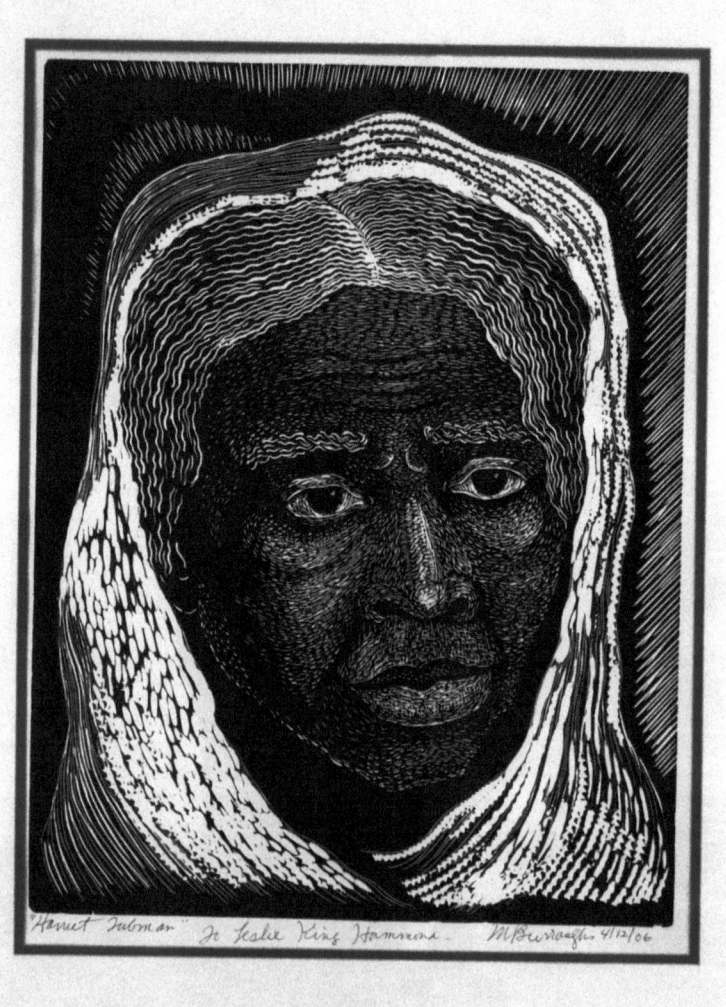

MARGARET BURROUGHS   Awarded in 1981
Harriet Tubman, n.d.
Lithograph, 18 x 24 in.
Private Collection

ELIZABETH CATLETT

Elizabeth Catlett (1915-2012) was a sculptor and printmaker known for her strong modernist depictions of figures expressive of the African-American experience and for her work for social justice, especially for African-American and Mexican women. She worked for many years in Mexico City.

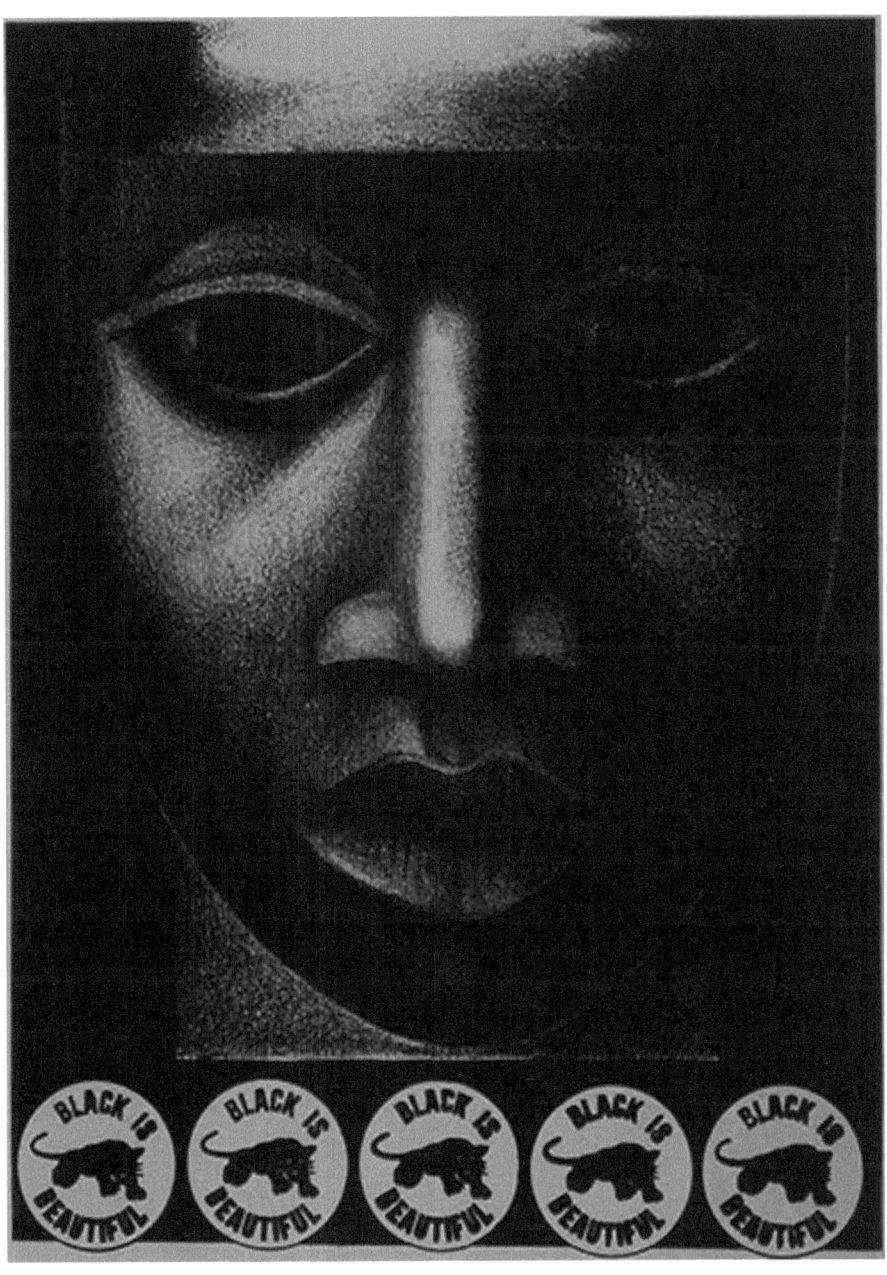

ELIZABETH CATLETT
Awarded in 1981
Black is Beautiful, n.d.
Lithograph, 18.5 x 13 in.
Courtesy of James E. Lewis Museum,
Morgan State University

BARBARA CHASE-RIBOUD

Barbara Chase-Riboud, (b. 1939) is a sculptor, poet, and author who lives in Rome and Paris. Her unique large-scale cast bronze and fiber sculptures on themes such as Malcolm X draw on African, Chinese, and modern western sources. Her prizewinning poetry and six historical novels include *Sally Hemmings* (1979).

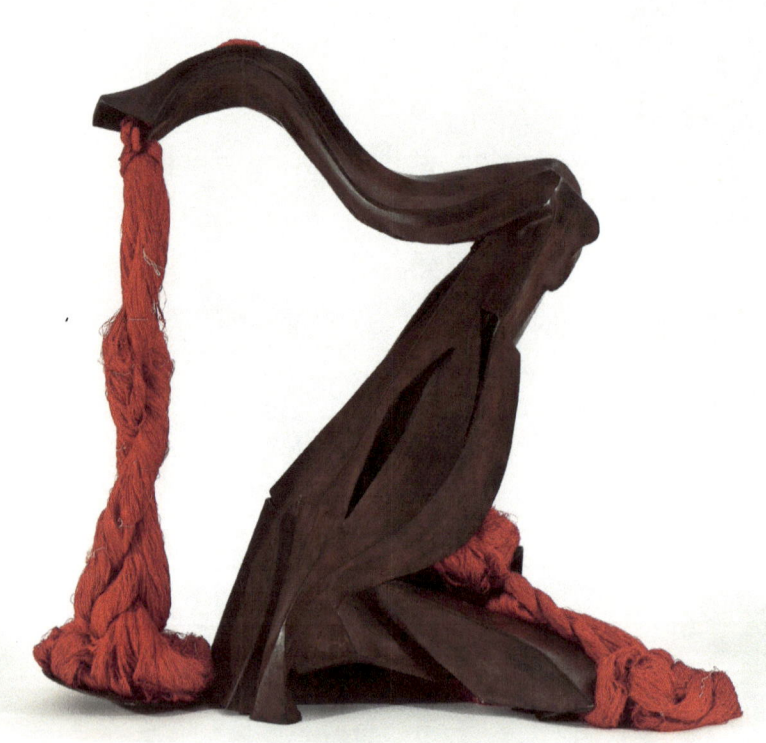

BARBARA CHASE-RIBOUD   Awarded in 2007
La Musica Red #4, 2003
Bronze with red patina and silk, 30 x 15 x 32 in.
Courtesy of Michael Rosenfeld Gallery LLC, New York NY

JUDY CHICAGO

Judy Chicago (b. 1939) is an artist, writer, educator, and feminist activist. She co-founded Womanhouse with Miriam Schapiro at Cal Arts and the Los Angeles Women's Building. Her *Dinner Party* (1974-1979) was created with the participation of hundreds of volunteers. Another collaborative project was the *Birth Project*.

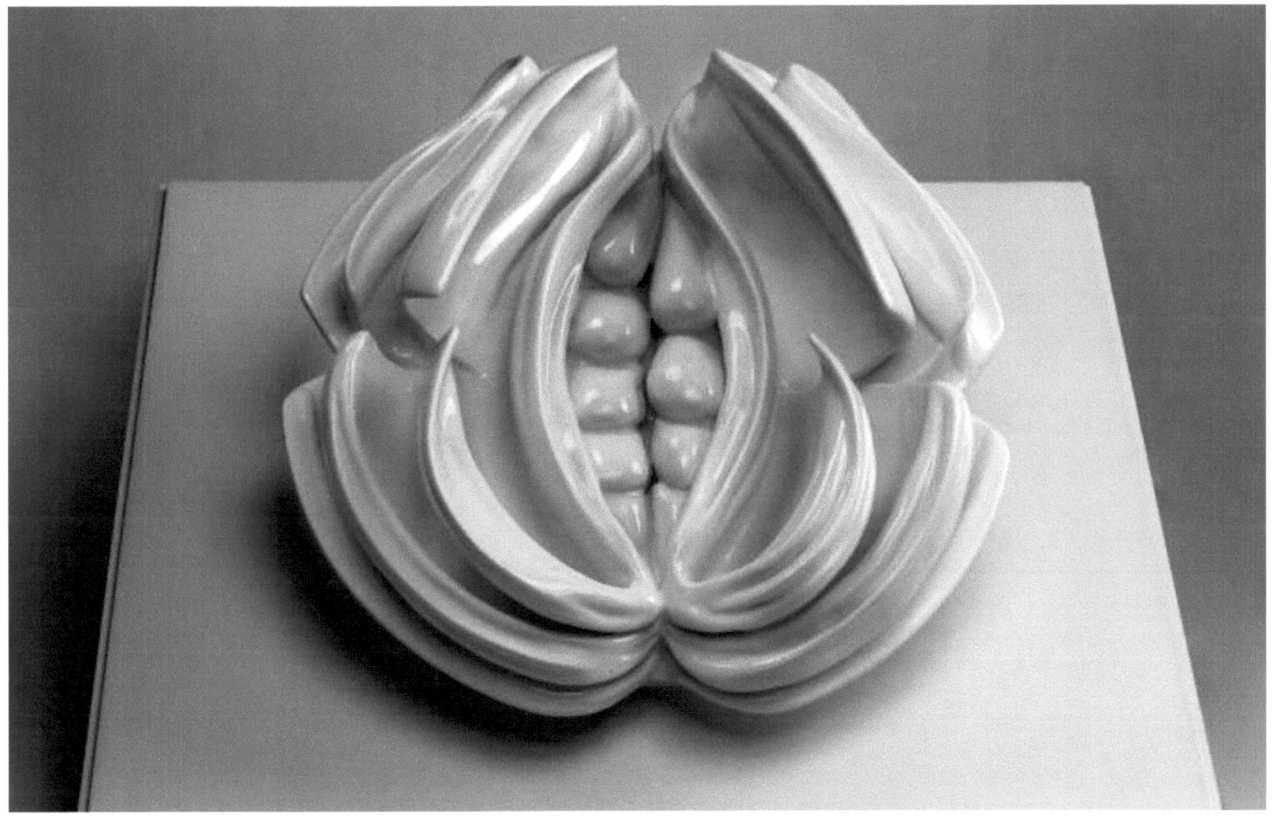

JUDY CHICAGO   Awarded in 1999
Virginia Wolf (Test Plate for "The Dinner Party"), 1978
Glazed porcelain, 14 in. diameter.
On loan from the National Museum of Women in the Arts,
Gift of Elizabeth A. Sackler in honor of Wilhelmina Cole Holladay

CLAIRE FALKENSTEIN

Claire Falkenstein (1908-1997) was a sculptor, painter, jewelry designer, and educator, who created thousands of works of art, including abstract public art that was at times controversial. Her innovative sculpture was often made of metal, glass, and resin, with pieces assembled in centralized or expanding configurations.

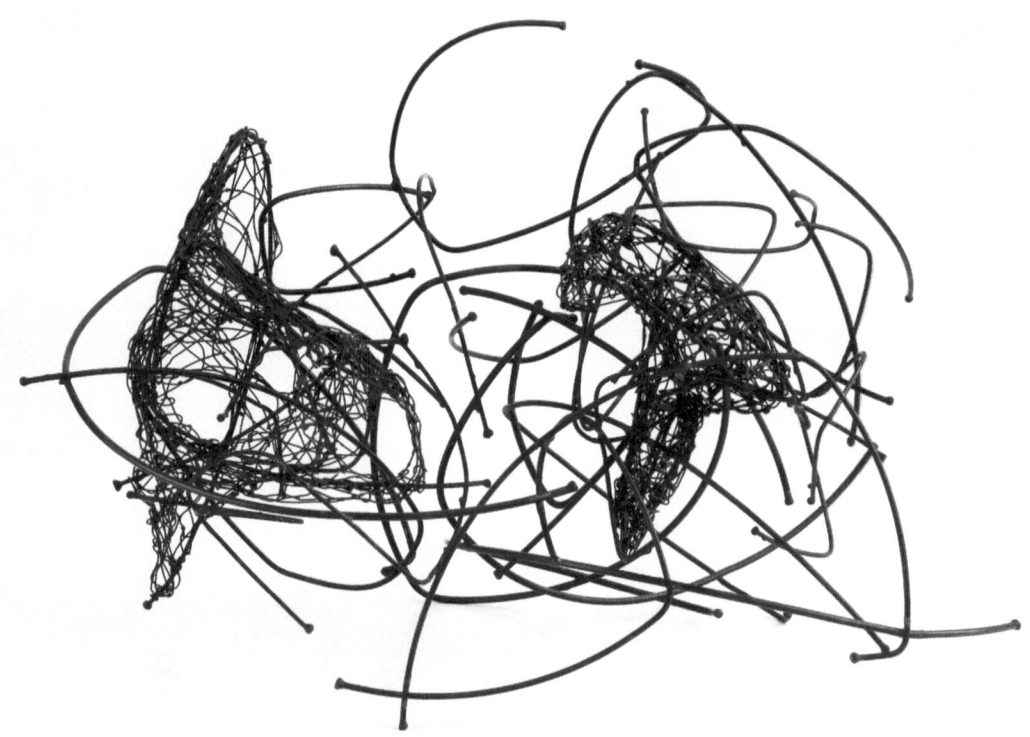

CLAIRE FALKENSTEIN   Awarded in 1981
Nid, 1958
Copper, 16.5 x 17 x 26 in.
©The Falkenstein Foundation
Courtesy of Michael Rosenfeld Gallery LLC, New York NY

SUE FULLER

Sue Fuller (1914-2006) was an innovative printmaker and sculptor. She created experimental textural prints and compositions of threads. She then moved to an original form of sculpture called String Compositions, made of threads stretched to create transparent geometric designs. Using newly developed plastic materials allowed her to pioneer imbedding clear threads in plastic.

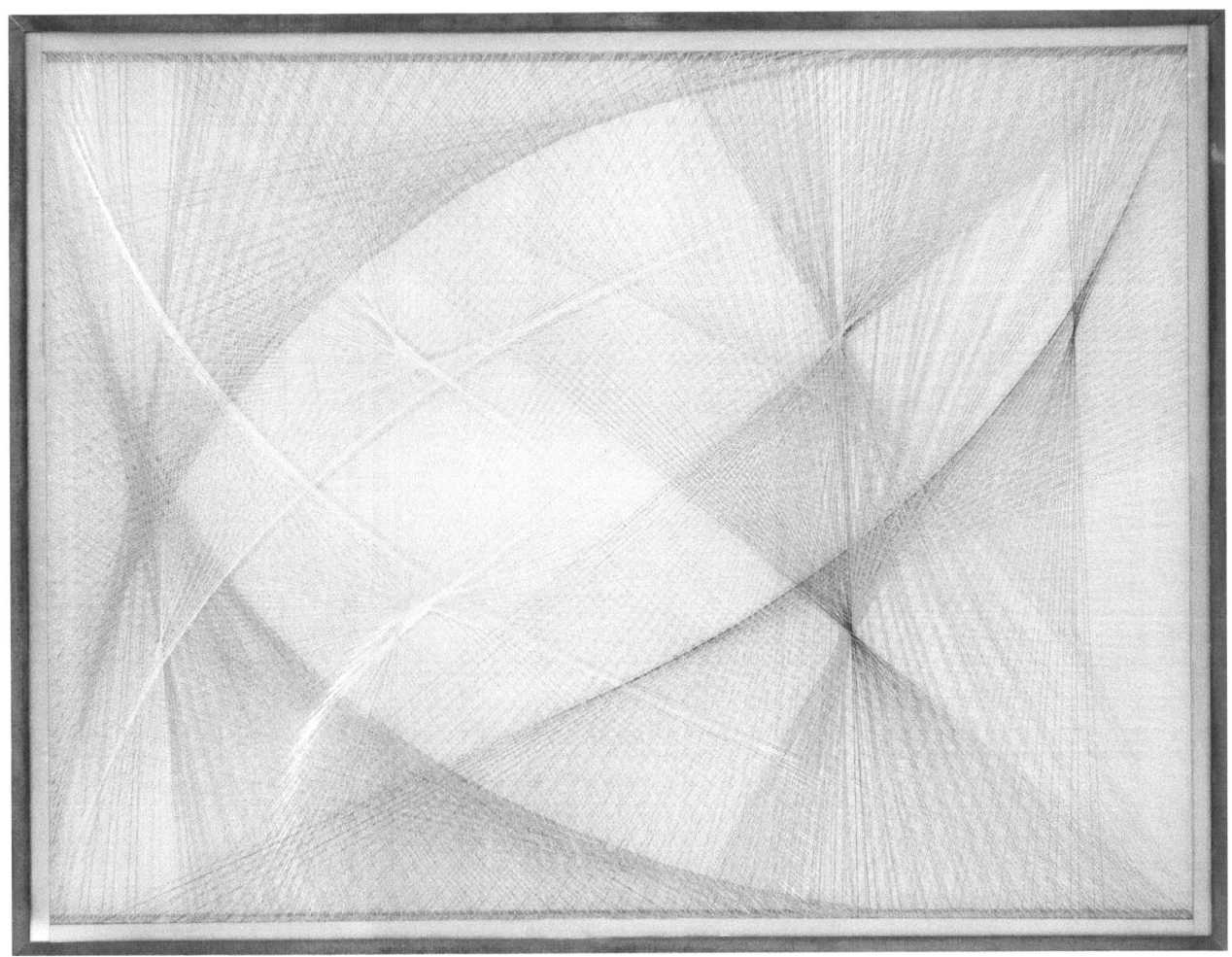

SUE FULLER   Awarded in 1986
String Construction #70, 1956
String construction over board in wood and steel box, 36.25 x
48.25 x 1.5 in.
Courtesy of Michael Rosenfeld Gallery LLC, New York NY

NANCY GRAVES

Nancy Graves (1939-1995) was a sculptor, painter, and filmmaker who invented new forms of sculpture in a wide range of materials. She was the first woman to have a solo exhibition at the Whitney Museum of American Art in 1969. She combined plant forms cast in bronze and found objects in her sculpture, which she painted in many colors. She explored topographical imagery in her paintings.

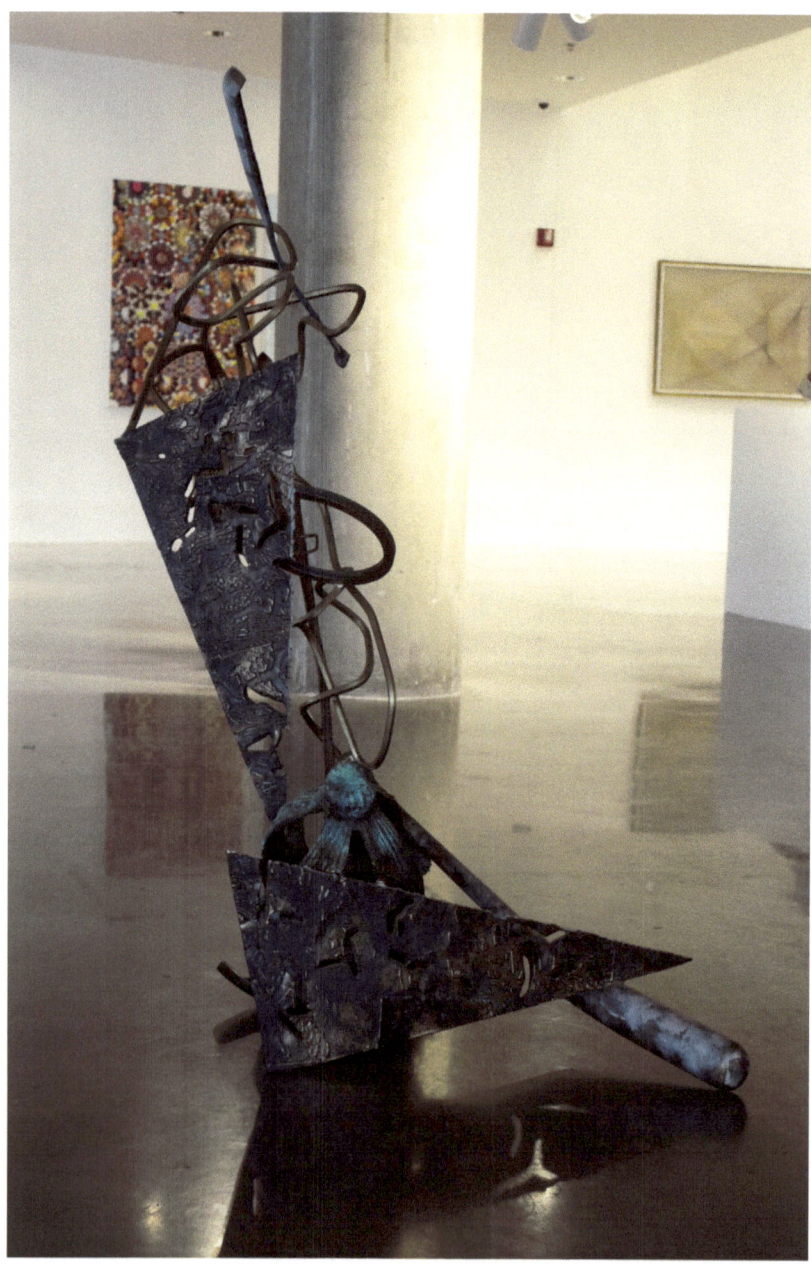

NANCY GRAVES   Awarded in 1993
Frisson of Fear, 1995
Bronze, 48.25 x 27 14 x 30.5 in.
Courtesy of American University Museum

NANCY GROSSMAN

Nancy Grossman (b. 1940) is a sculptor best known for her carved heads and bodies made of wood and covered with sewn and zippered black leather. She is also known for her bold dyed-paper collage pastels of torsos. Her works, which she called autobiographical, often appear savage, nightmarish, and sexually charged, invoking themes of power and restraint.

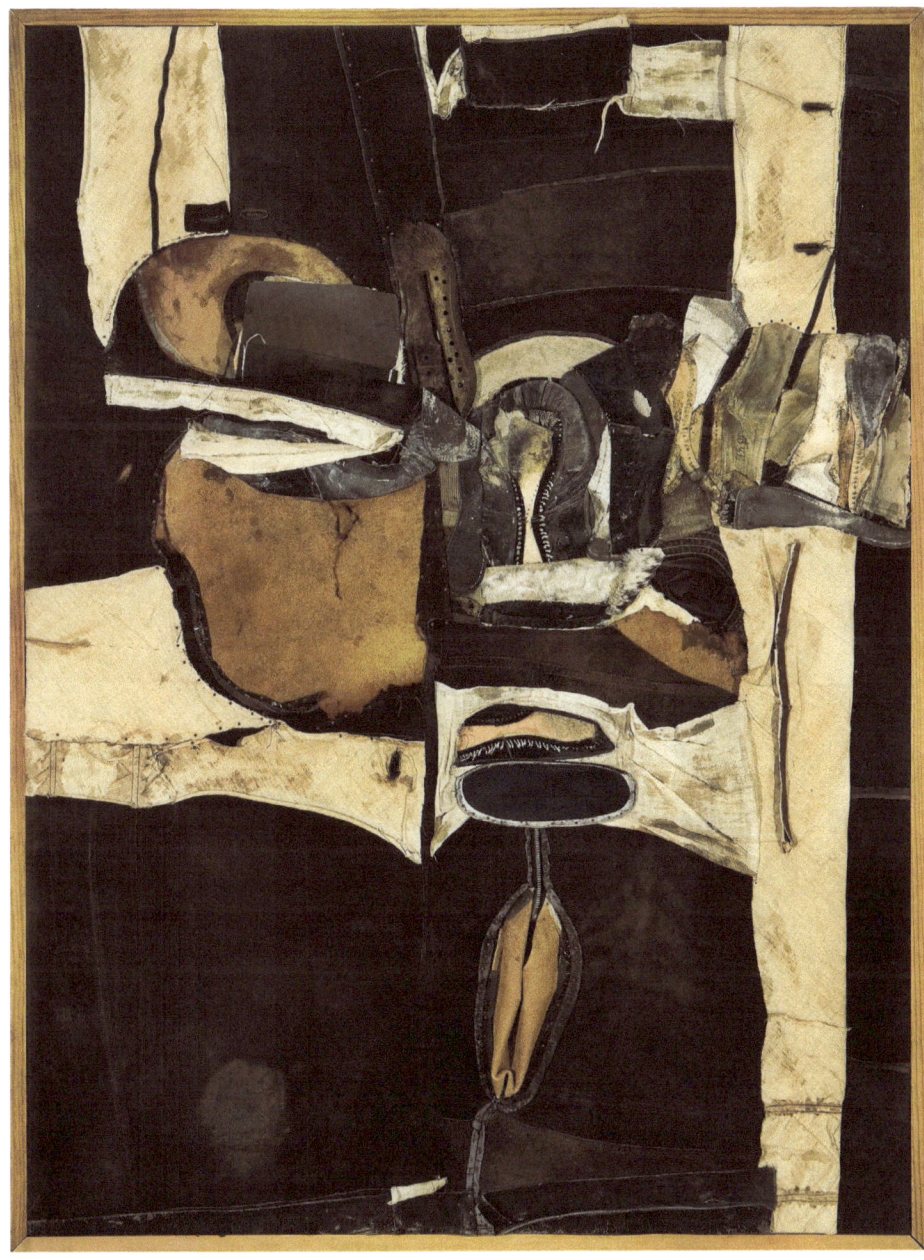

NANCY GROSSMAN
Awarded in 2008
Black Landscape, 1964
Leather, fabric, metal, wood, fur, bristle, paper, nylon, and paint assemblage mounted to plywood, 49.875 x 38 x 3.5 in.
Courtesy of Michael Rosenfeld Gallery LLC, New York NY

GRACE HARTIGAN

Grace Hartigan (1922-2008) was a painter and educator who was a leading female artist of the second generation of New York Abstract Expressionists. Her work bridged Pop Art with her introduction of representational imagery, inspired by Old Masters, billboards, magazine ads, and store fronts, rendered in boldly applied color.

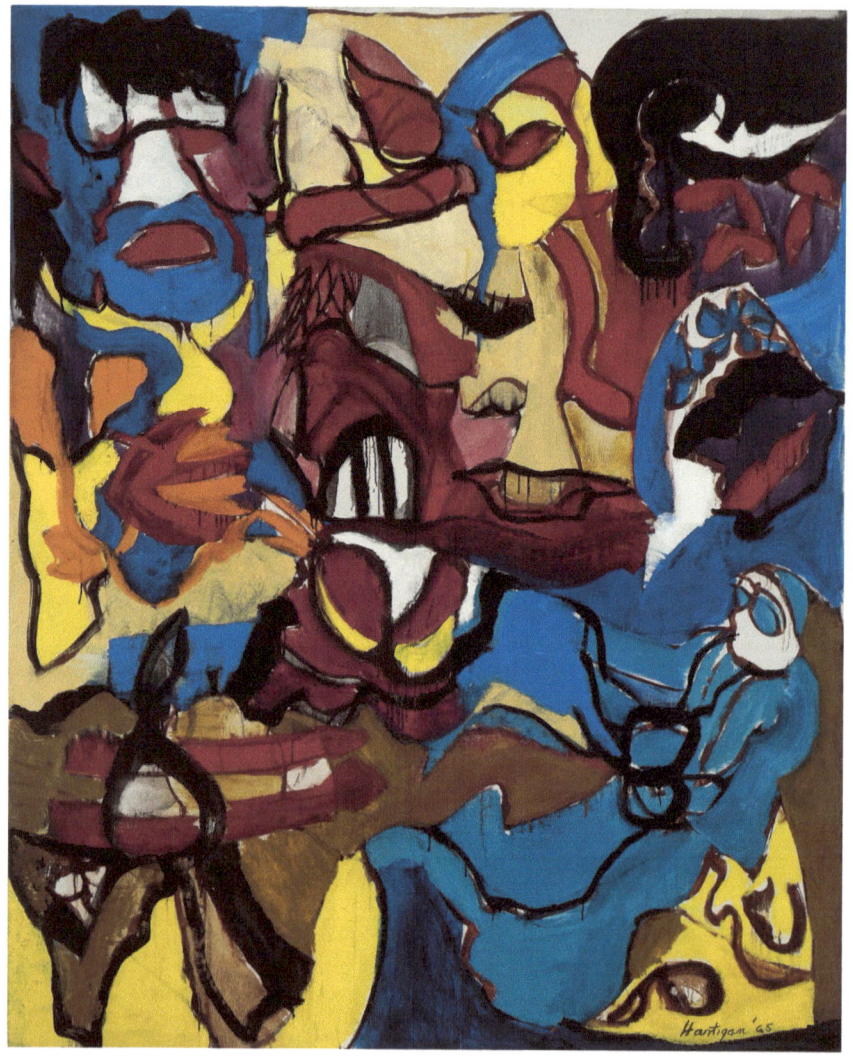

GRACE HARTIGAN Awarded in 1987
Trick or Treat, 1965
Oil on canvas, 72.25 x 60.125 in.
Courtesy of Michael Rosenfeld Gallery LLC, New York NY

MAREN HASSINGER

Maren Hassinger (b. 1947) is a multimedia artist and educator who creates sculpture, installation, performance, and video art, experimenting with artistic materials and invoking nature. She has served as the Director of the Rinehart School of Sculpture at Maryland Institute College of Art in Baltimore, MD since 1997.

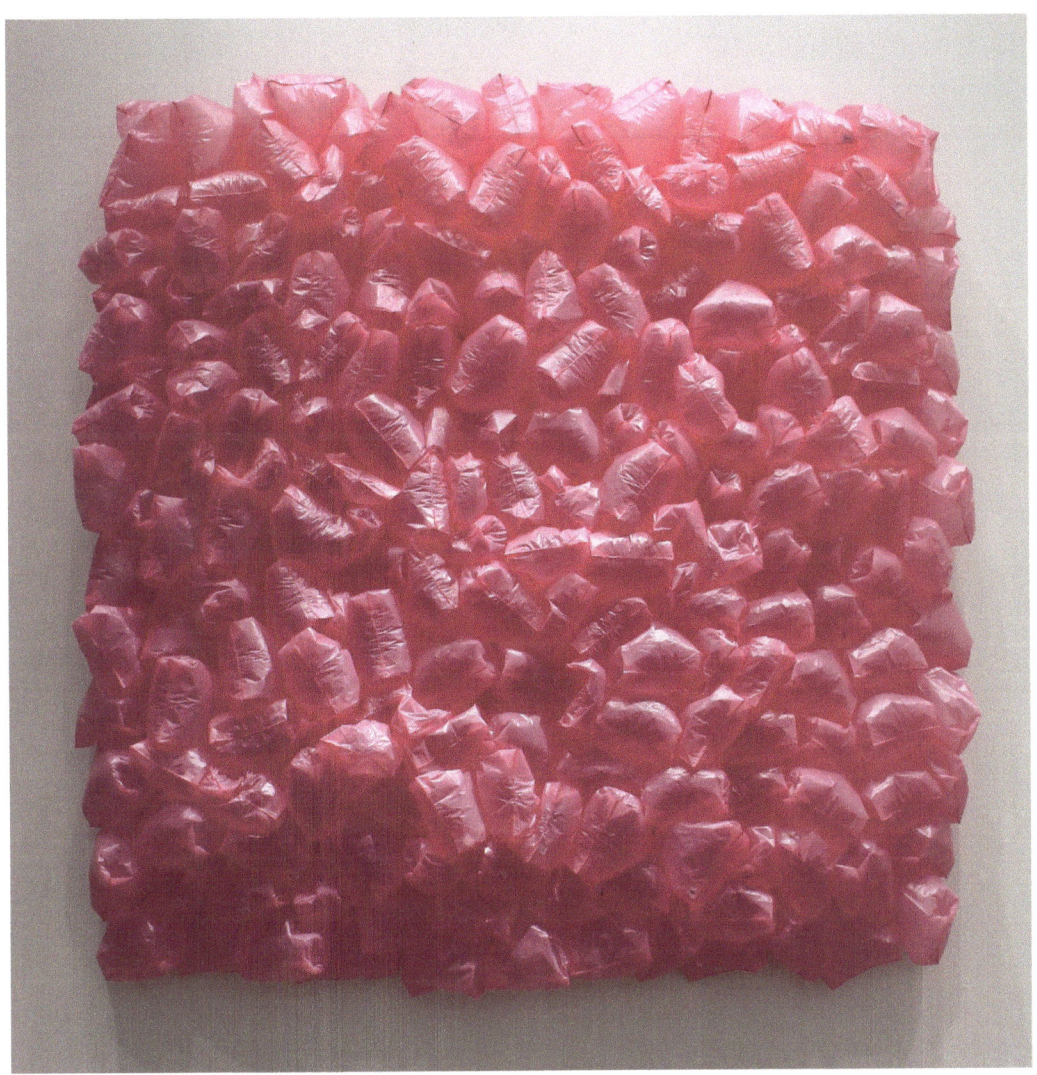

MAREN HASSINGER   Awarded in 2009
Love, 2009
Pink plastic bags, dimensions vary
Courtesy of the Reginald F. Lewis Museum

LOÏS MAILOU JONES

Loïs Mailou Jones (1905-1998) was a painter, textile designer, graphic artist, writer, and educator based in Washington, DC, whose brilliantly colored paintings were strongly influenced by time in Paris and Haiti. Paintings of African masks and textile patterns evoked African-American heritage. She taught design and watercolor at Howard University for almost half a century (1930-1977).

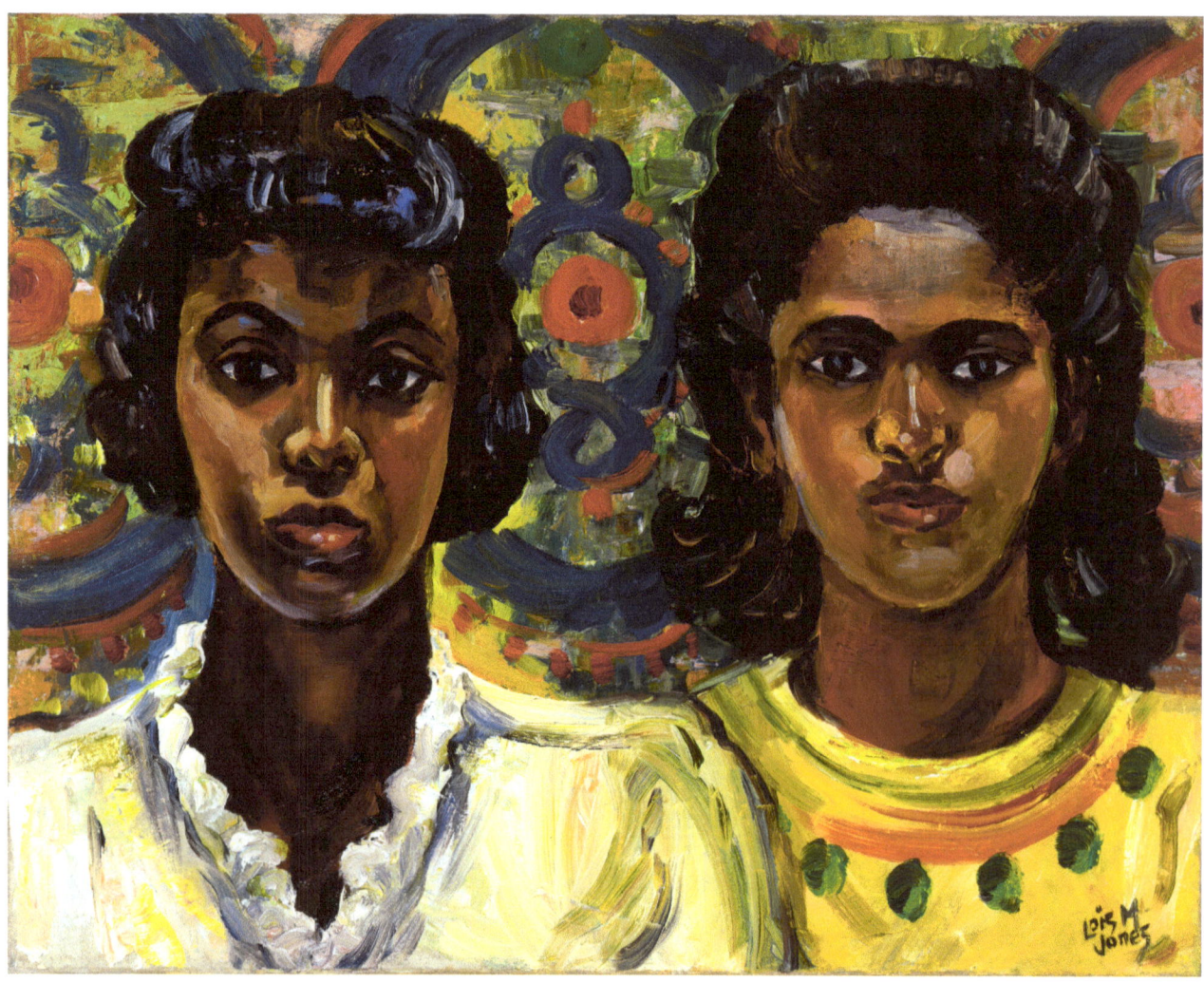

LOIS MAILOU JONES   Awarded in 1986
Two Women, 1950
Oil on linen, 16.25 x 21 in.
Courtesy of Michael Rosenfeld Gallery LLC, New York NY

JOYCE KOZLOFF

Joyce Kozloff (b. 1942) is an artist, activist, critic, and educator based in Los Angeles whose artistic process focuses on "infinite variation" and the potential of pleasure. Her groundbreaking work contributed to the Pattern and Decoration movement. Her work ranges from public architectural installations to ceramics, collage, and frescoes.

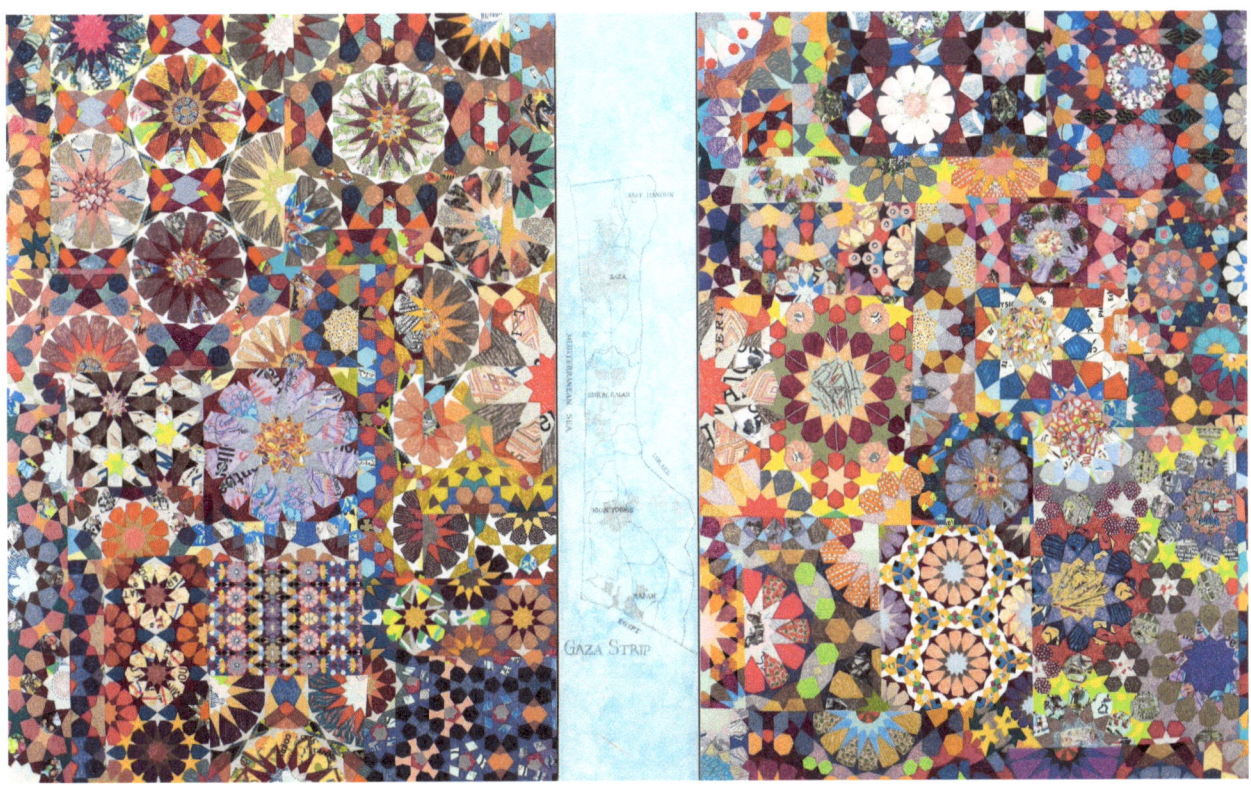

JOYCE KOZLOFF   Awarded in 2009
If I Were a Botanist (Gaza), 2015
Mixed media on canvas, 54 x 91.25 in.
Courtesy of DC Moore Gallery

LEE KRASNER

Lee Krasner (1908-1984) was a painter who was part of the first generation of Abstract Expressionists. For six decades as an artist, she created innovative forms of abstraction balanced with figuration and of all over painting. She moved to large canvases and is known for the striking collages made from cut-up old paintings.

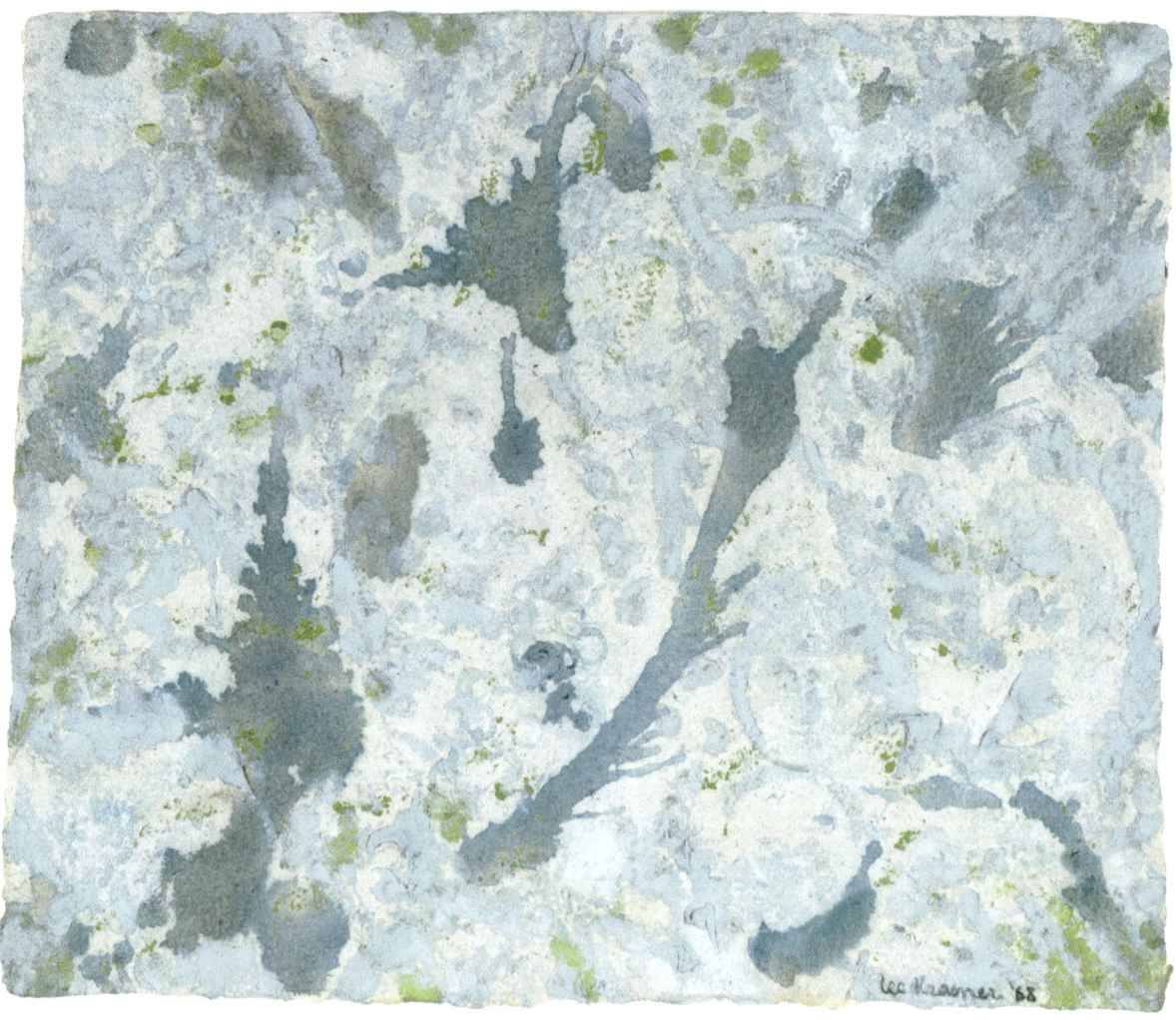

LEE KRASNER Awarded in 1980
Water No. 2, 1968
Gouache on Douglas Howell paper, 18 x 22 in.
Courtesy of Michael Rosenfeld Gallery LLC, New York NY

SAMELLA SANDERS LEWIS

Samella Sanders Lewis (b.1924) is a painter, printmaker, art historian, and educator, known as a historian and collector of African-American art. She founded an international journal about art by descendants of Africans. Dr. Lewis has numerous exhibitions, films, and books to her credit, including the first afro-centric book on African-American art.

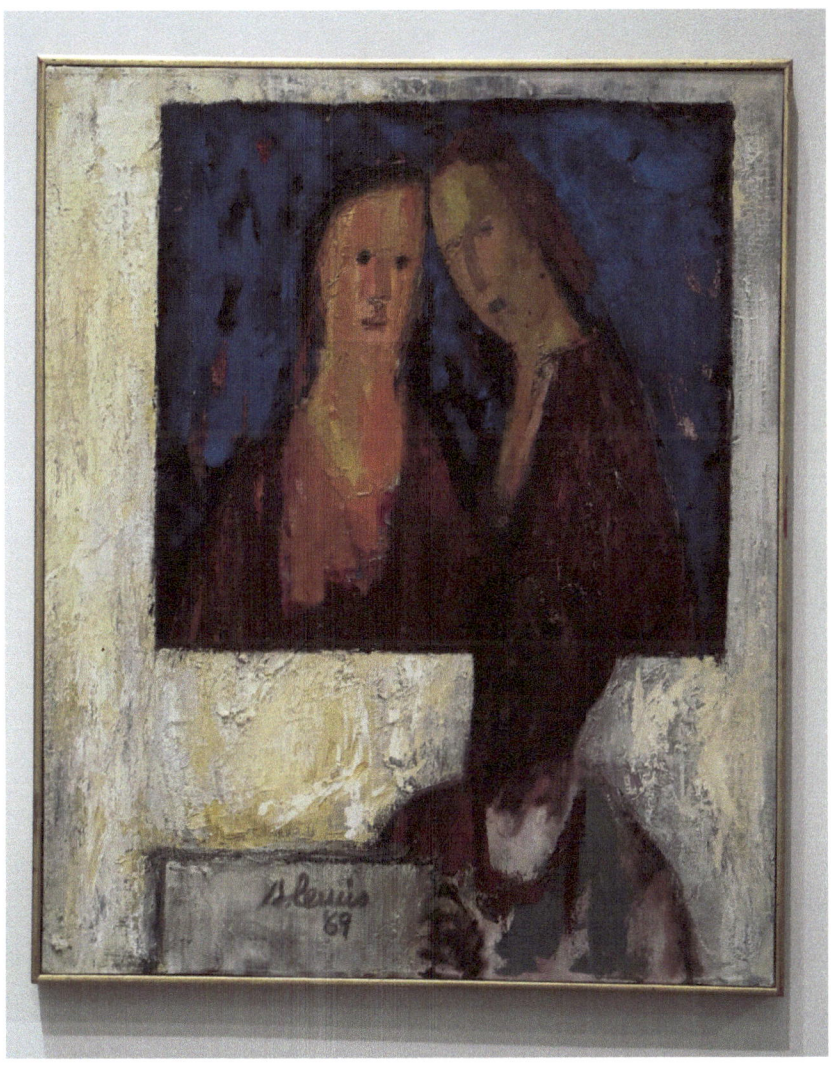

SAMELLA SANDERS LEWIS Awarded in 1989
White House, 1969
Oil on canvas, 36 x 30 in.
Courtesy of Dr. Diane Whitfield Locke and John Woo

EVANGELINE J. MONTGOMERY

Evangeline Montgomery (b. 1933) is a mixed-media artist, printmaker, and curator who coordinated exhibitions seen internationally. She promoted several California artists and brought attention to black women artists in her area. While working for the U.S. Information Agency in Washington, DC, she developed inclusive and expansive traveling exhibitions of American art.

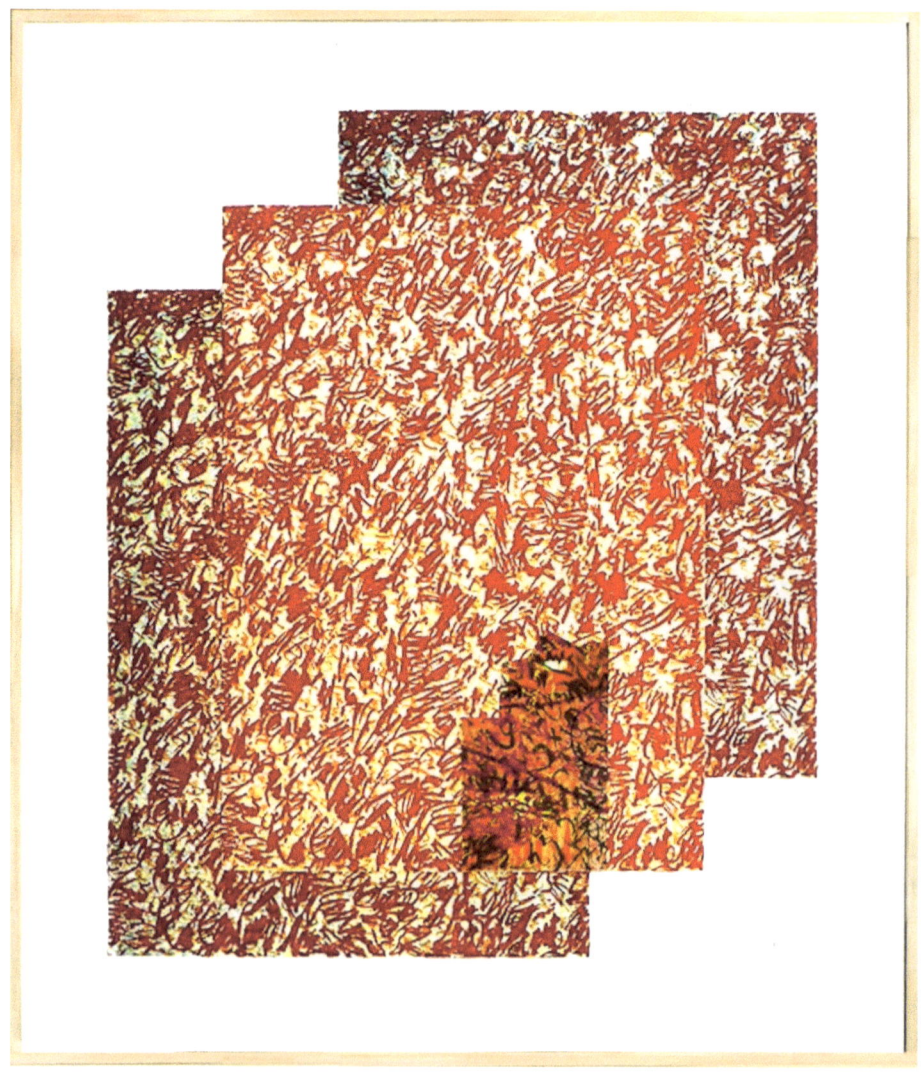

EVANGELINE J. MONTGOMERY   Awarded in 1999
In Memory of Martin, n.d.
Mixed media print, 47.5 x 43.5 in.
Courtesy of James E. Lewis Museum, Morgan State University

BEVERLY PEPPER

Beverly Pepper (b.1924) is a sculptor working on a monumental scale in welded steel, often creating site specific, environmental, and land art for international locations. Although made of industrial materials, her "Earthbound Sculptures" seem to emerge from the earth. Although abstract in form, her columns and urban altars suggest mythical and symbolic meaning.

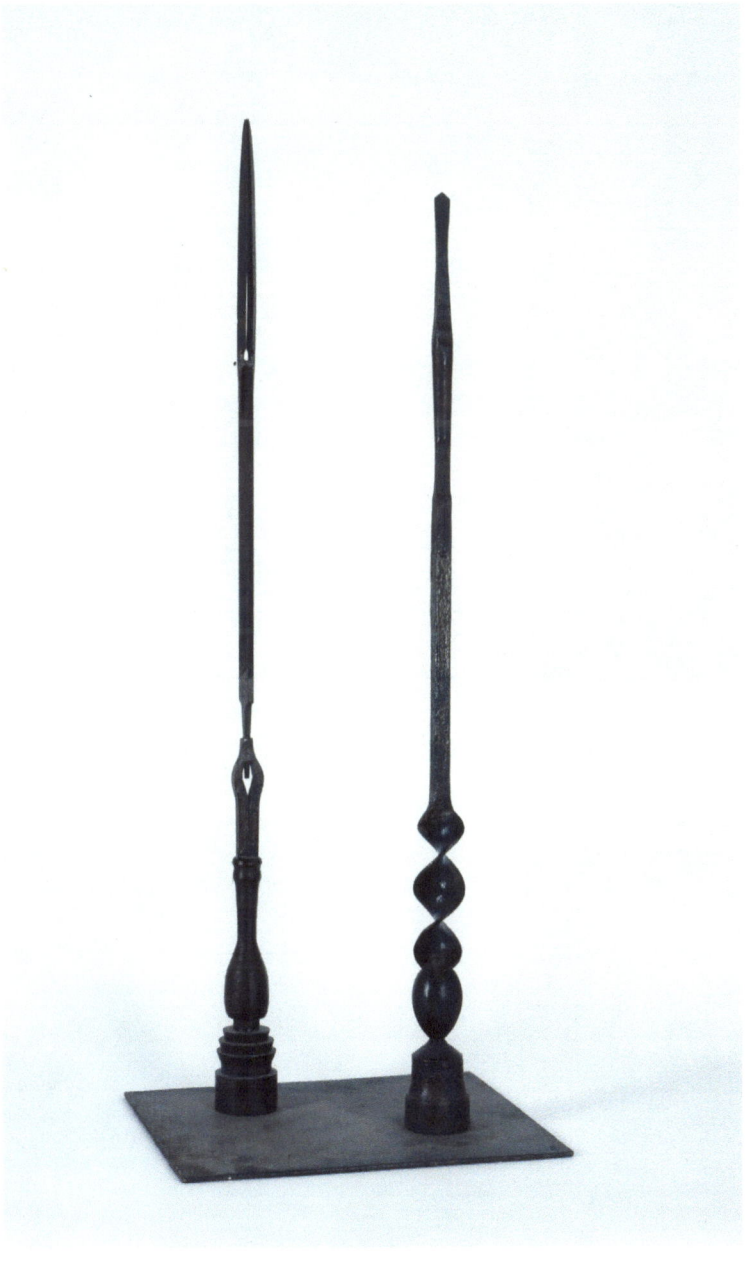

BEVERLY PEPPER   Awarded in 1994
Untitled, 1980
Welded steel objects, 35.5 x 13.875 x 11.875 in.
Courtesy of Michael Rosenfeld Gallery LLC,
New York NY

FAITH RINGGOLD

Faith Ringgold (b. 1930) is a quilter, painter, sculptor, performance artist and activist in the field of African-American and Women's rights. Much of her artwork in the early sixties portrayed the civil rights movement from the female perspective. She is the recipient of more than 75 awards, including 22 Honorary Doctor of Fine Arts Degrees.

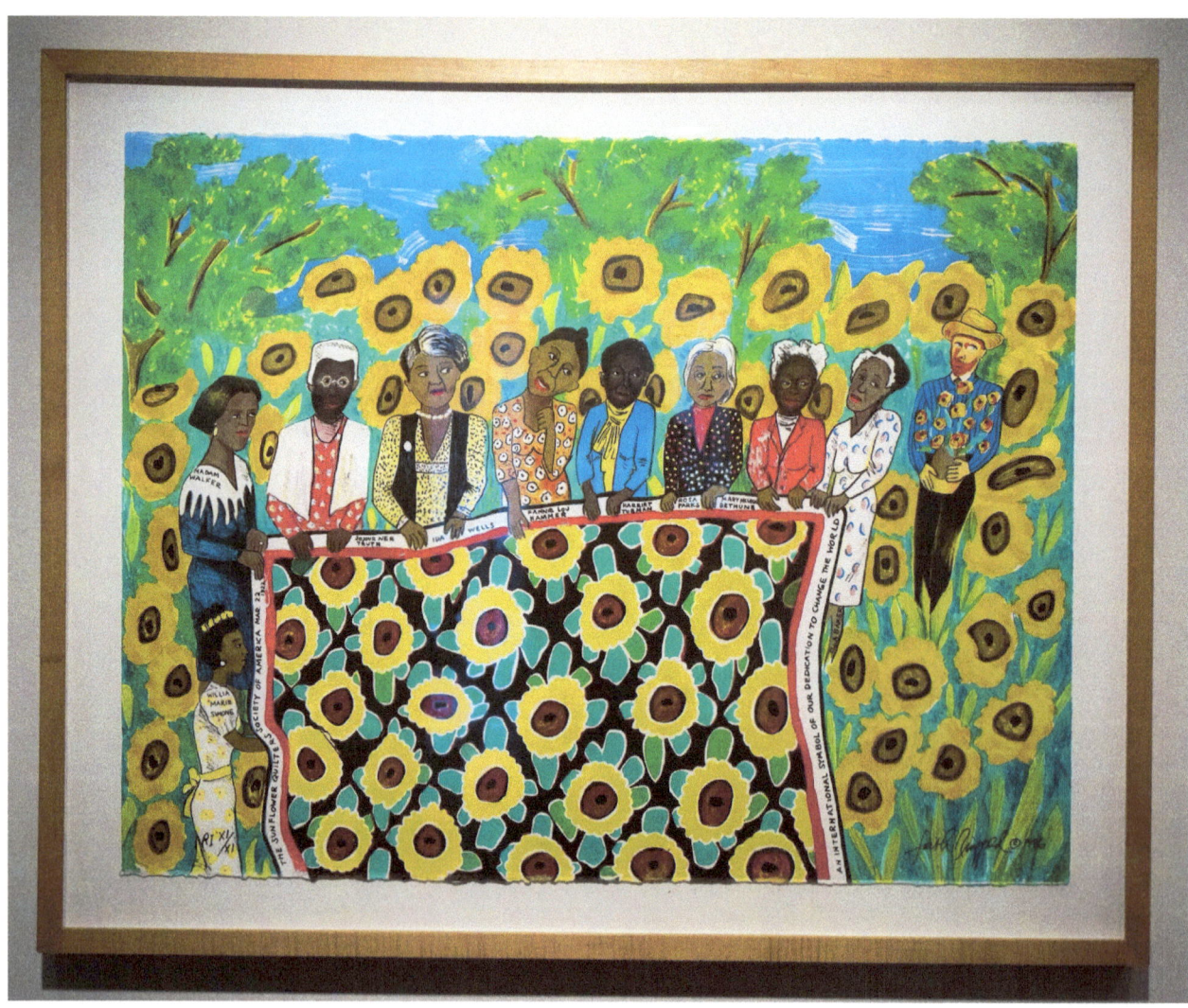

FAITH RINGGOLD   Awarded in 1994
The Sunflower Quilting Bee at Arles, 1995
Lithograph, 22 x 30 in.
Published as benefit print for CAA by the Brodsky Center
Courtesy of Judith K. Brodsky

BETYE SAAR

Betye Saar (b.1926) is an artist and educator who has challenged negative images, perceptions, and oppression of African-Americans. She protested stereotyped images and objects by incorporating them into her collages and assemblages. Later work references African tribal objects and African-American and family history and grew to room-size installations.

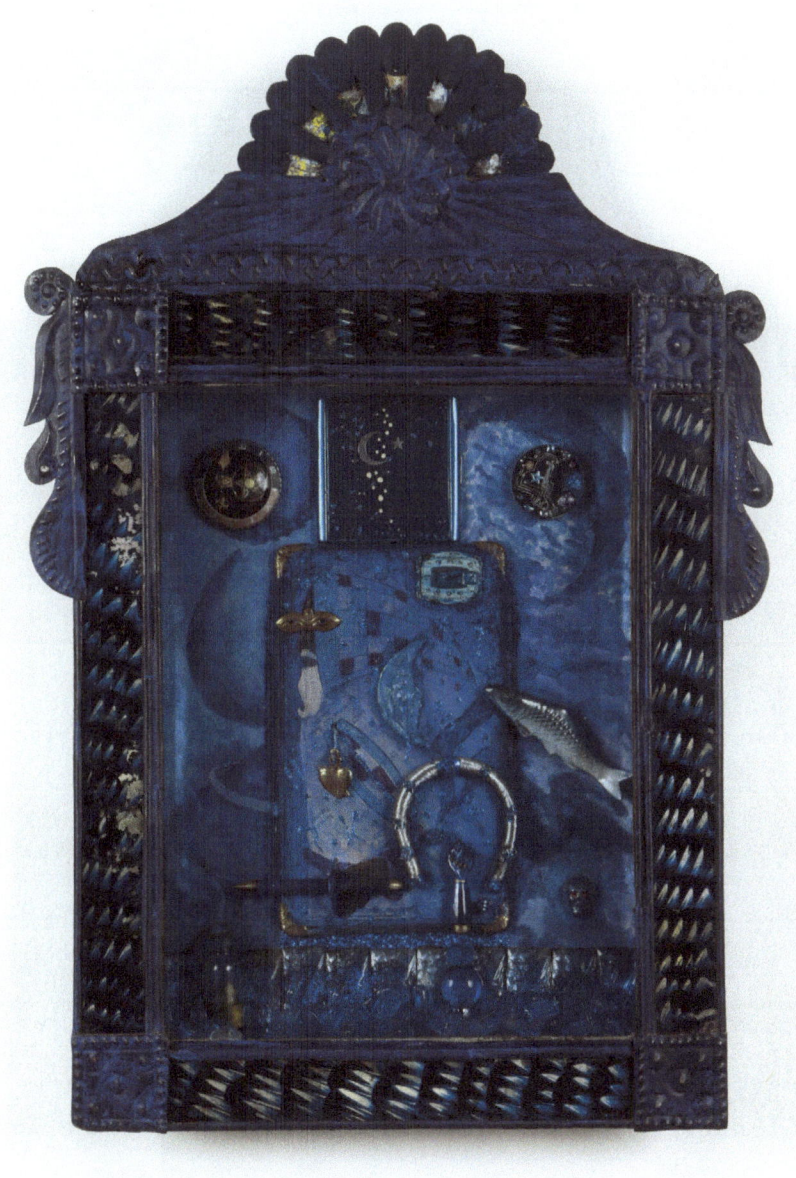

BETYE SAAR   Awarded in 1989
Blue Moon Neptune, 1989
Mixed media assemblage, 17 x 12 x 1.5 in.
Courtesy of Michael Rosenfeld
Gallery LLC, New York NY

MIRIAM SCHAPIRO

Miriam Schapiro (1923-2015) was a pioneering feminist artist and educator and part of the Pattern and Decoration movement. With Judy Chicago she created the Feminist Art Program at the California Institute of the Arts and the installation Womenhouse. She moved from hard-edged abstractions to incorporating fabric into the paintings she called femmages.

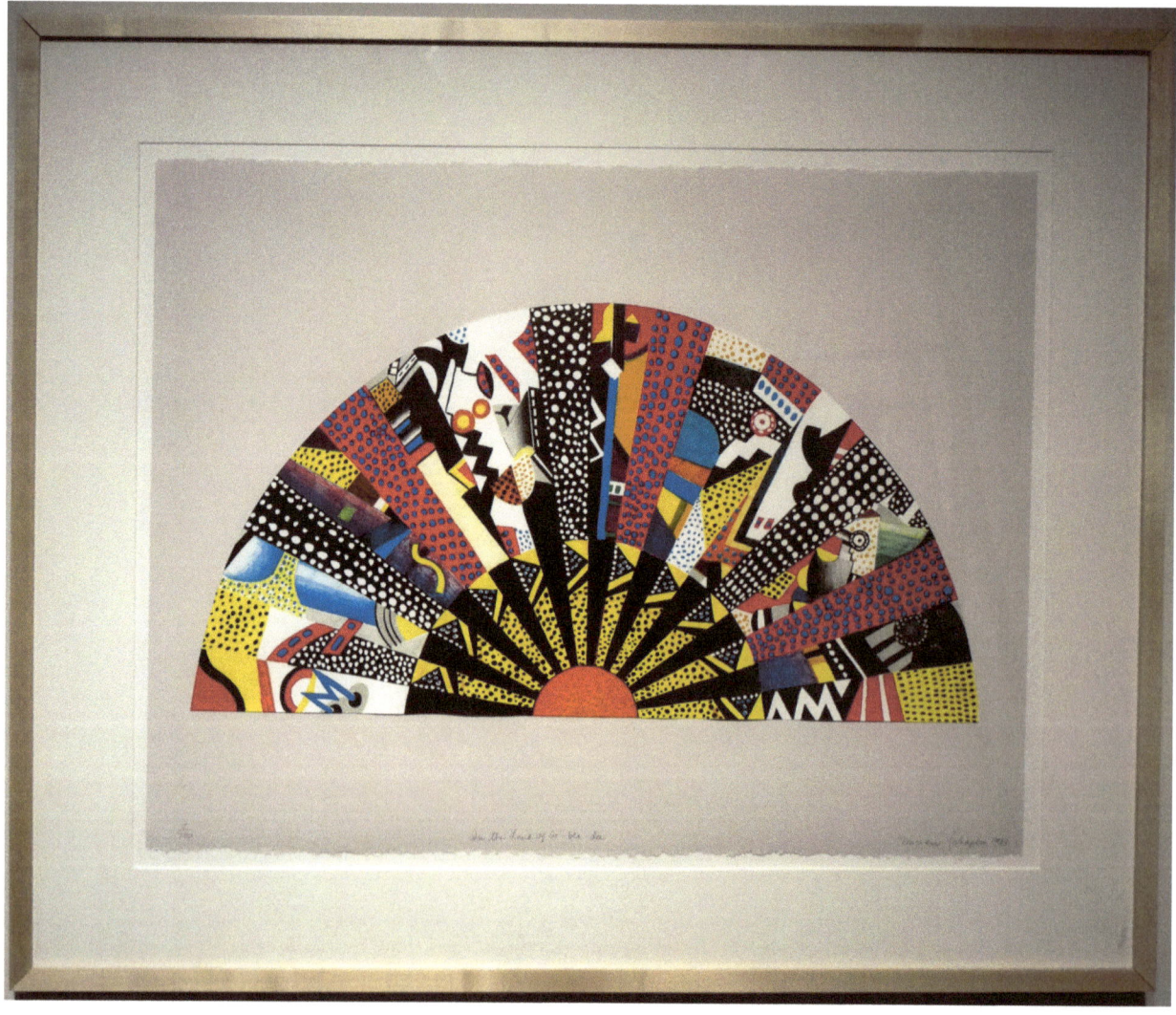

MIRIAM SCHAPIRO   Awarded in 1988
In the Land of Oo-Bla-Dee, 1993
Mixed media silk screen print, 22 x 30 in.
Published as benefit print for CAA by the Brodsky Center
Courtesy of Judith K. Brodsky

JOYCE J. SCOTT

Joyce J. Scott (b. 1948), Baltimore jewelry artist, sculptor, printmaker, performance artist, and educator, uses free-form woven beaded sculptures and neckpieces to form provocative images. Drawing on craft traditions of her African-American, Native American, and Scottish heritage, she includes found objects to enhance her messages against racism, sexism, and injustice.

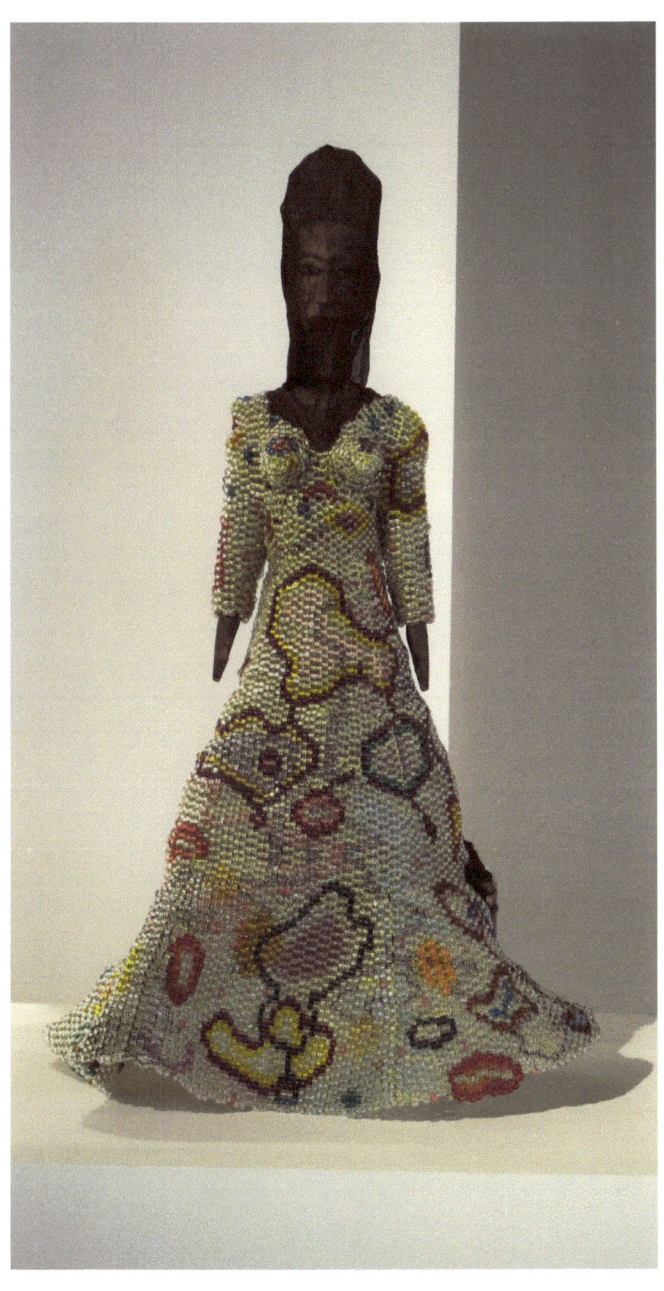

JOYCE SCOTT   Awarded 2010
Pretty Girl Veiled, 2012
Nigerian wood object, plastic and glass beads, thread, and fabric, 44 x 24 x 26 in.
Courtesy of Goya Contemporary Baltimore

ELIZABETH TALFORD SCOTT

Elizabeth Talford Scott (1916-2011) was a textile artist known for her innovative free-form quilts. She learned quilt-making from her parents but enhanced hers with embroidery, beads, found objects, and story content. Her quilts were exhibited in and collected by art museums. Her daughter Joyce J. Scott is also an awardee.

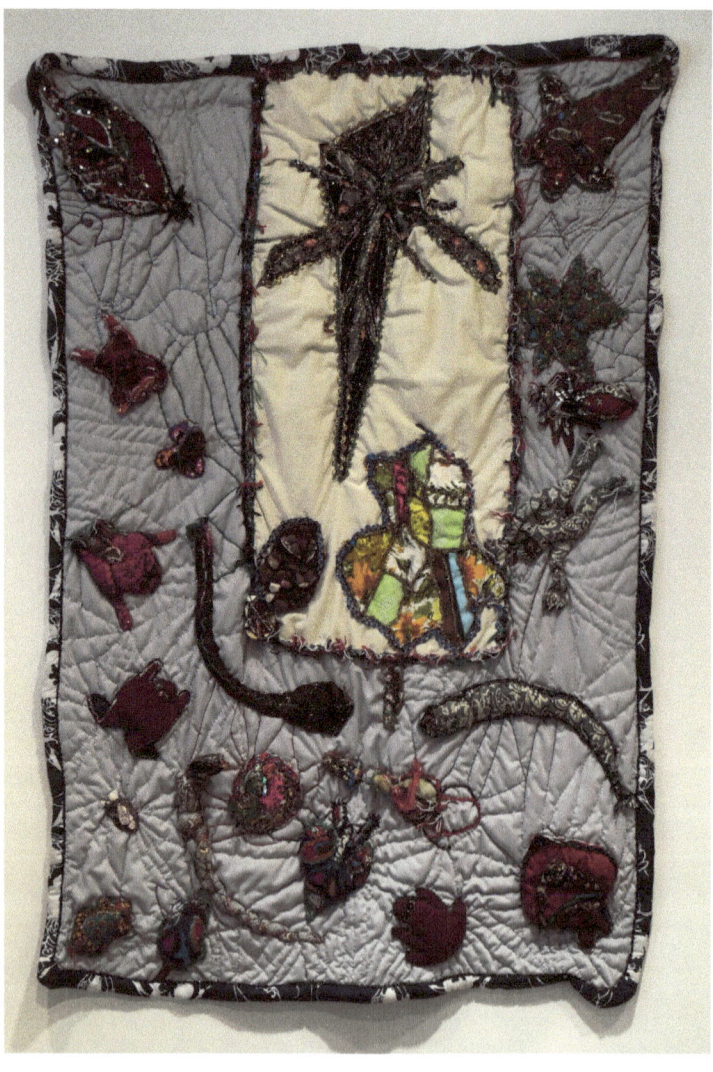

ELIZABETH TALFORD SCOTT   Awarded in 1987
Voyage to the Bottom of the See, 1992
Fabric, thread, ricks, beads, buttons, shells, 69 x 57 in.
Private Collection

SYLVIA SLEIGH

Sylvia Sleigh (1916-2010) was a painter known for her realist still lifes, landscapes, and portraits of her contemporaries. She turned the tables by painting life-size portraits of nude men, valuing personality and intellect as well as the body. She was part of A.I.R. Gallery and feminist groups, and promoted other women artists.

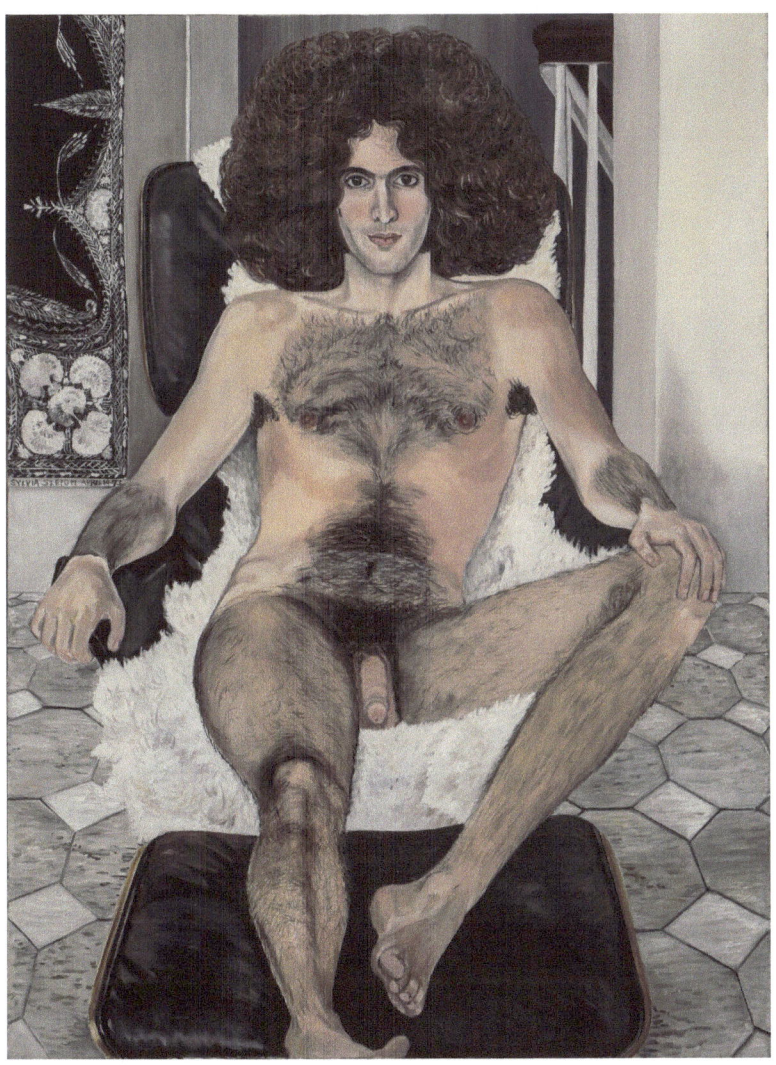

SYLVIA SLEIGH   Awarded in 2011
Paul Rosano, Seated Nude, 1973
Oil on canvas, 56 x 42 in.
On loan from the National Museum of Women in the Arts
Gift of Mr. and Mrs. Russell Bowman

NANCY SPERO

Nancy Spero (1926-2009) was an artist and activist who was an early feminist, member of Art in Revolution and founding member of A.I.R. Gallery. Her figurative art is inspired by ancient art and mythology. Often times, she expressed her rage against injustice, violence, and war, in the form of painted and collaged scrolls.

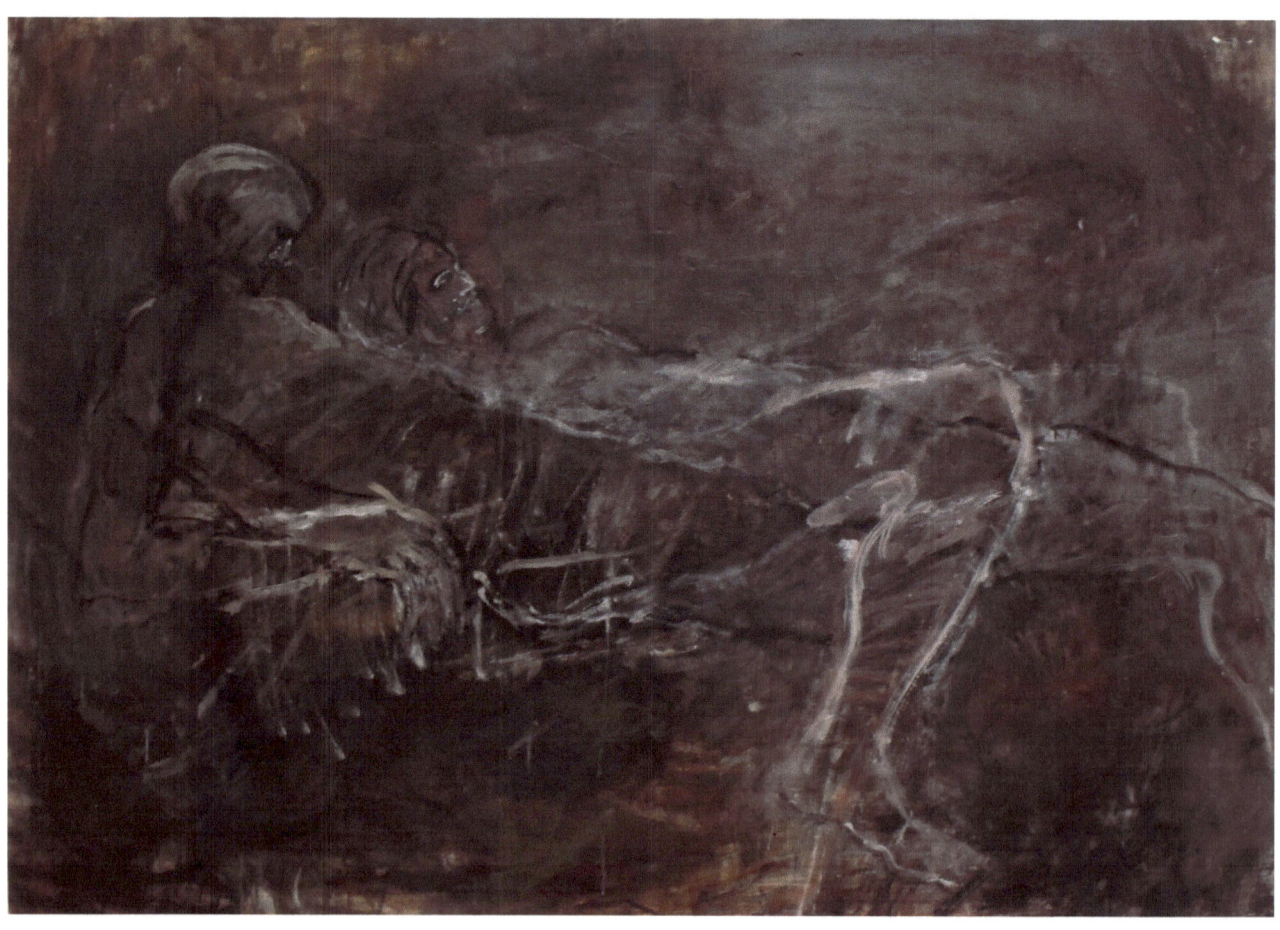

NANCY SPERO   Awarded in 2003
Lovers, 1963
Oil on canvas, 55 ½ x 80 1/2 in.
Courtesy of Michael Rosenfeld Gallery LLC, New York NY

LENORE TAWNEY

Lenore Tawney (1907-2007) was an influential fiber artist who transformed the flat surface of weaving into three dimensions. Her ground breaking sculptural works, which she called "woven forms," were constructed of colorful yarns and floated freely in space as seen in her Cloud Series, commissions for public buildings.

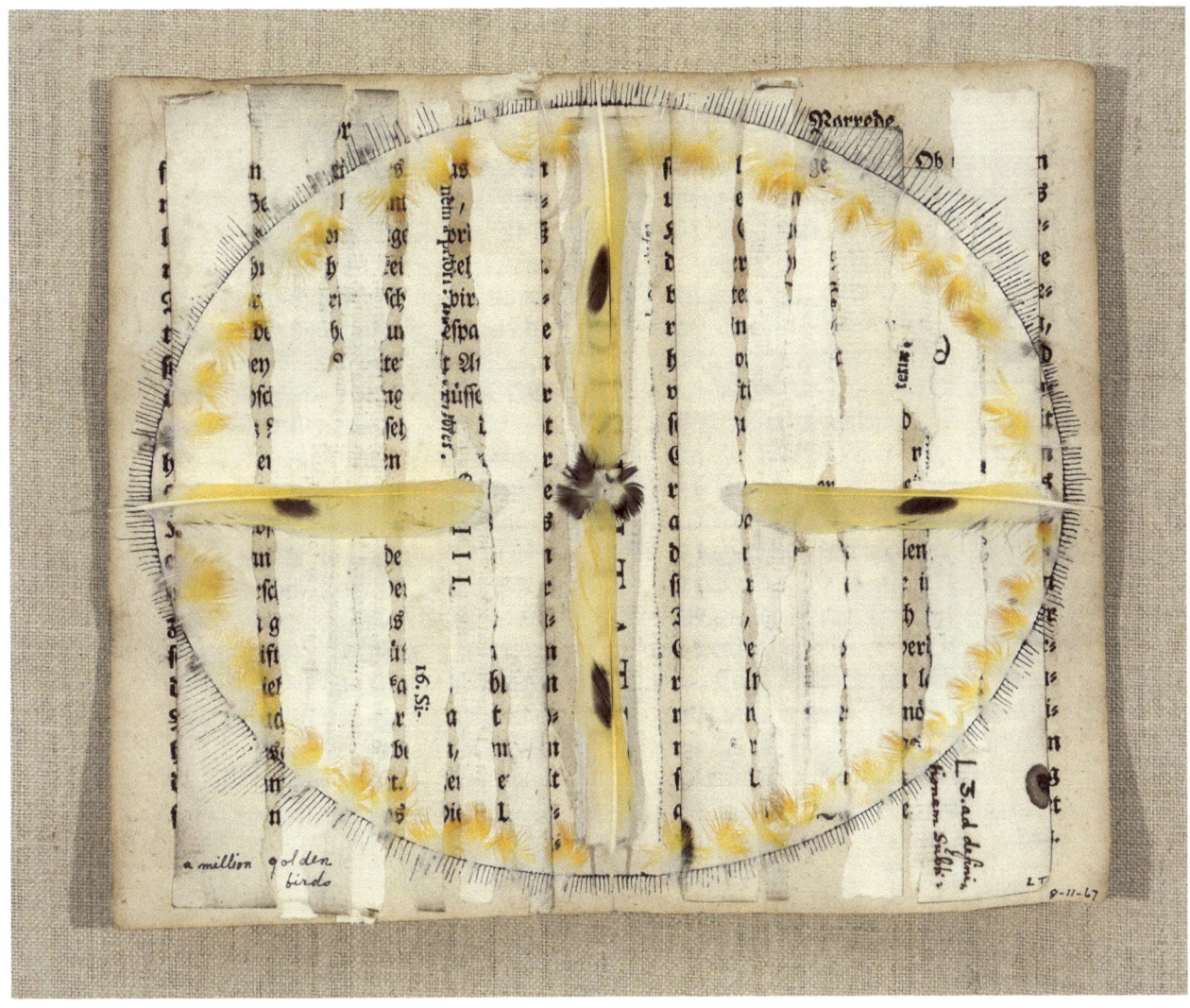

LENORE TAWNEY   Awarded in 1983
A Million Golden Birds, 1967
Mixed media collage of printed and cut papers with feathers,
6.875 x 10.125 x .5 in.
Courtesy of Michael Rosenfeld Gallery LLC, New York NY

CHARMION VON WEIGAND

Charmion von Wiegand (1896-1983) was an abstract painter and journalist whose art and ideas on spirituality were influenced by her friend Piet Mondrian, Theosophy, tantric yoga, and Tibetan Buddhism. Her paintings were often composed of geometric forms in pure color, reflecting her metaphysical theories.

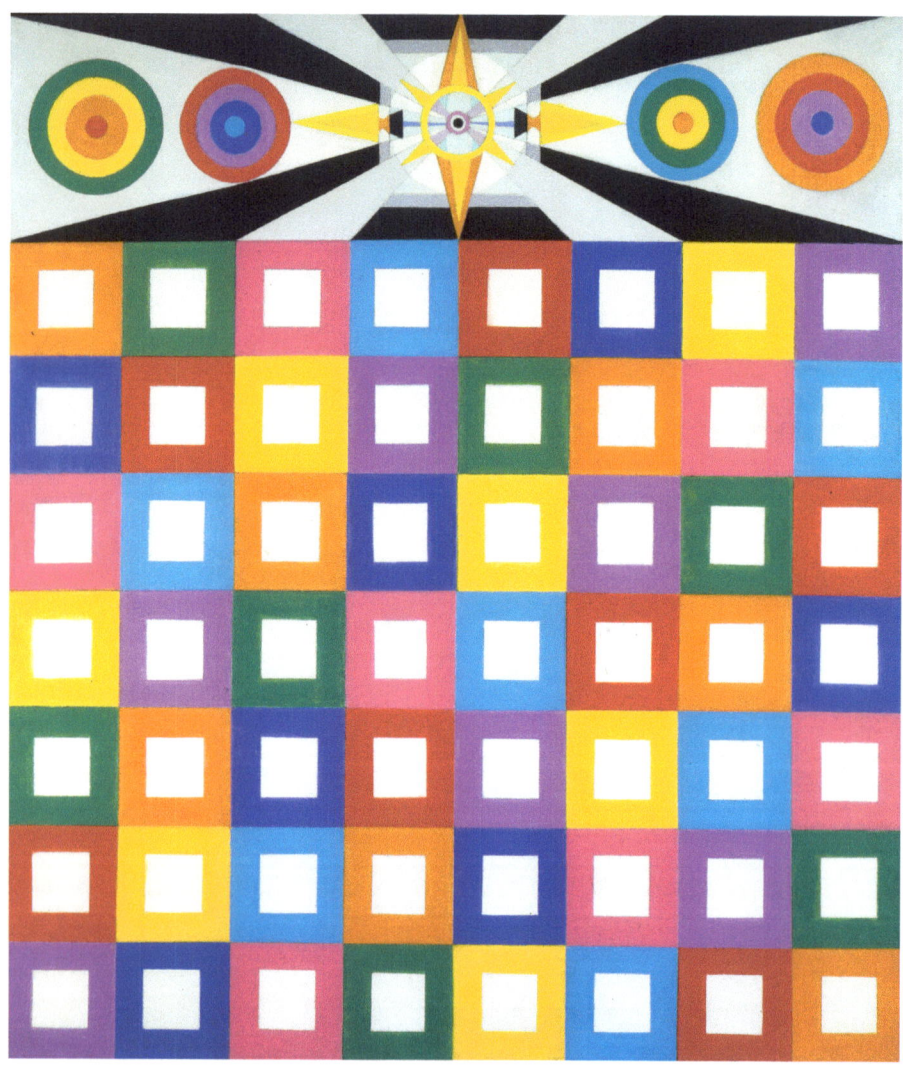

CHARMION VON WEIGAND   Awarded in 1982
the Paradise Gambit, 1964-65
Oil on canvas, 45 x 40 in.
Courtesy of Michael Rosenfeld Gallery LLC, New York NY

RUTH WEISBERG

Ruth Weisberg (b. 1942) is printmaker, educator, writer, critic, and curator whose artwork reflects stories, struggles, desires and her commitment to her Jewish family heritage. She was the President of the College Art Association (1990-1992) and Dean of the University of Southern California's Roski School of Fine Arts (1995-2010).

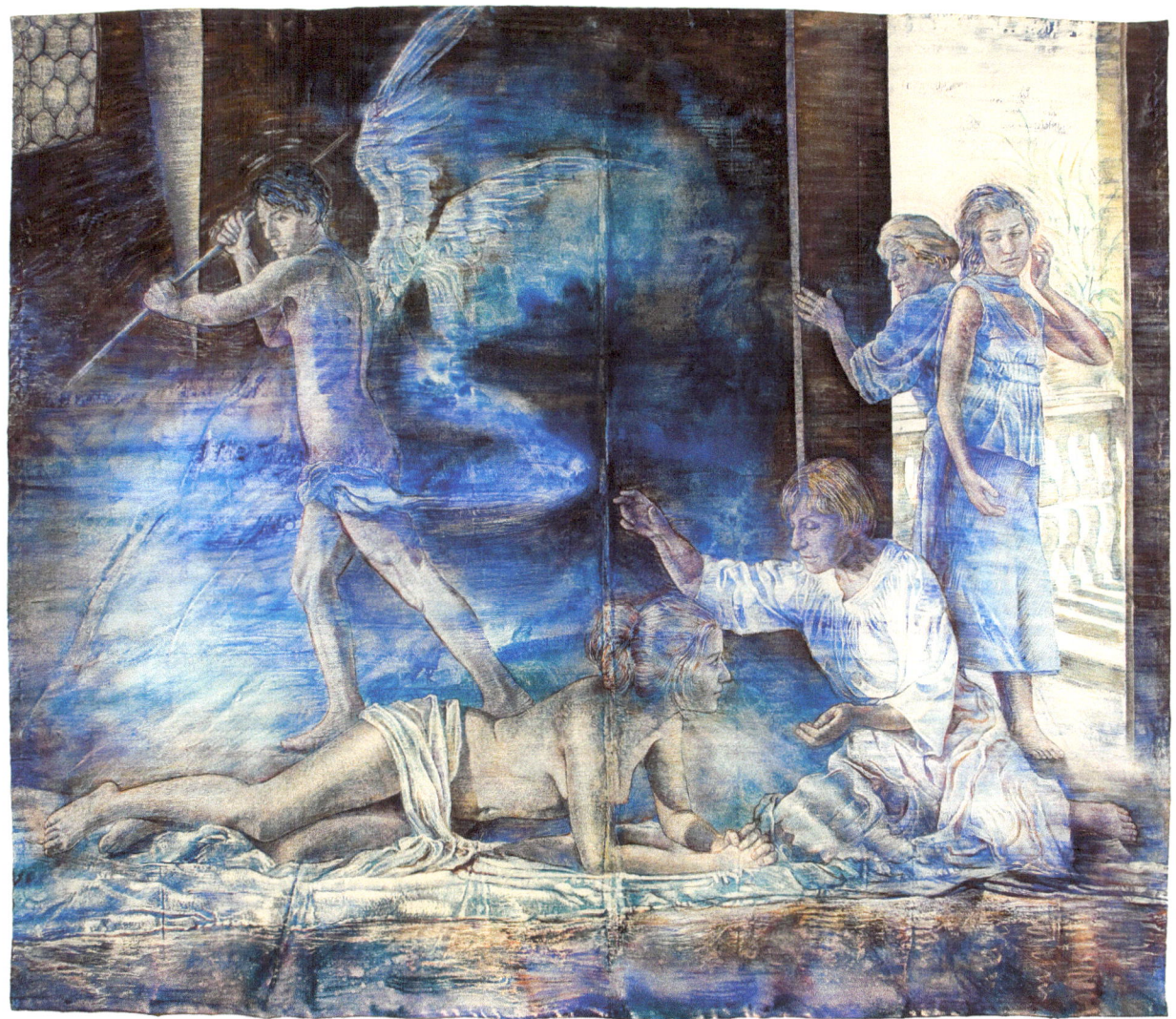

RUTH WEISBERG   Awarded in 2009
The Blessing, n.d.
Oil, mixed media on canvas, 80 x 96 in.
Courtesy of Jack Rutberg Fine Arts

CLAIRE ZEISLER

Claire Zeisler (1903-1991) was a pioneer fiber artist. She moved from weaving to create off-the-loom knotted and threaded large sculptural forms, usually made of natural materials. She was inspired by modern and tribal African art and ancient Peruvian and American Indian textiles and baskets to create a new form of fiber art.

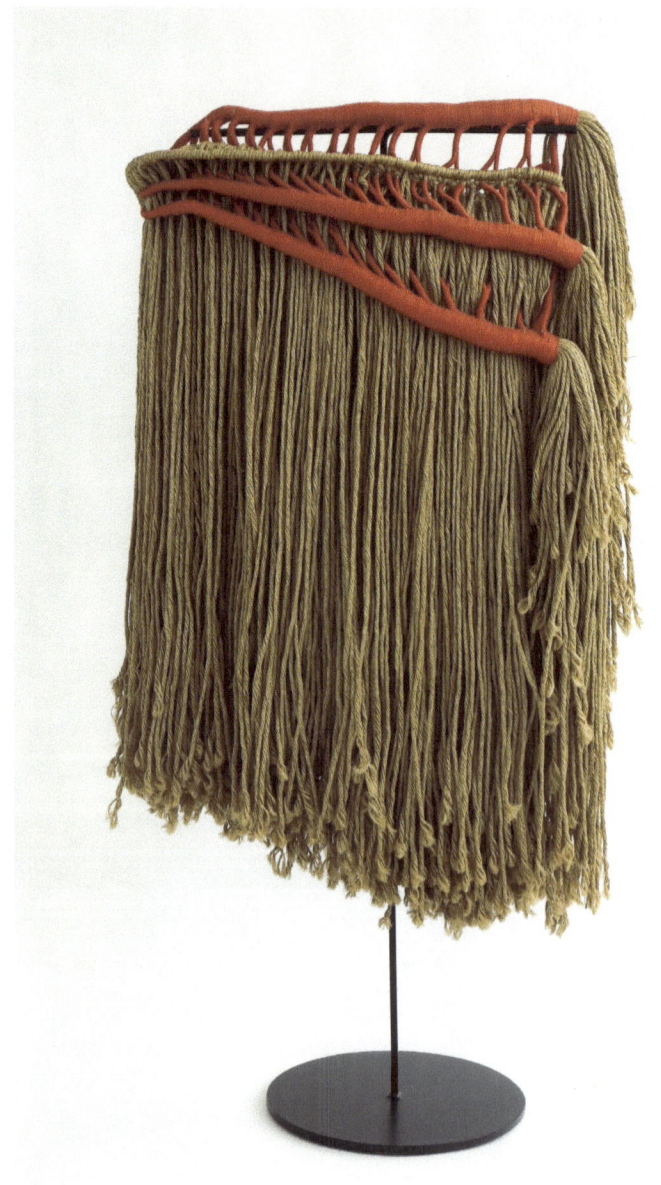

CLAIRE ZEISLER Awarded in 1982
Untitled, c. 1975
Colored and natural fiber construction with painted metal base, 49.25 x 24.5 x 10 in
Courtesy of Michael Rosenfeld Gallery LLC, New York NY

CHECKLIST

HELÈNE AYLON Awarded in 2016
Bridge of Knots II, 2006
Video, 6 min 17 seconds,
Video documentation of the 2006 American University Museum
facade installation with audio by Meredith Monk
Courtesy of the Artist

ISABEL BISHOP Awarded in 1979
Walking in the Subway Station, 1963
Oil on board, 24 x 33 in.
Courtesy of Michael Rosenfeld Gallery LLC, New York NY

JUDITH BRODSKY Awarded in 2002
Dishrag Diagrammatic, 1978
Intaglio and relief, 20 x 20 in.
Published by Queenston Press for first UN Year of the Woman
Courtesy of Judith K. Brodsky

BEVERLY BUCHANAN Awarded in 2011
Shack, 1988
Wood and nails, 43 x 30 x 17 in. (house)
33 x 31 x 17 in. (table support)
Courtesy of Reginald F. Lewis Museum

SELMA BURKE Awarded in 1979
Family, c. 1950
Bronze, 42.375 x 14 x 15.25 in.
Courtesy of Michael Rosenfeld Gallery LLC, New York NY

DIANE BURKO Awarded in 2011
Peterman Heading South (after NASA), 2010-2011, 2012
Oil on canvas, 88 x 50 in.
Courtesy of the Artist

MARGARET BURROUGHS Awarded in 1981
Harriet Tubman, n.d.
Lithograph, 18 x 24 in.
Private Collection
ELIZABETH CATLETT Awarded in 1981
Black is Beautiful, n.d.
Lithograph, 18.5 x 13 in.
Courtesy of James E. Lewis Museum, Morgan State University

ELIZABETH CATLETT Awarded in 1981
Pensive, n.d.
Bronze, 19 x 10.25 x 11 in.
Courtesy of James E. Lewis Museum, Morgan State University

BARBARA CHASE-RIBOUD   Awarded in 2007
Anna Akhmatova Monument, St. Petersburg, 1996
Charcoal, charcoal pencil, and ink with engraving
and aquatint on paper, 31.5 x 23.75 in.
Courtesy of Michael Rosenfeld Gallery LLC, New York NY

BARBARA CHASE-RIBOUD   Awarded in 2007
La Musica Red #4, 2003
Bronze with red patina and silk, 30 x 15 x 32 in.
Courtesy of Michael Rosenfeld Gallery LLC, New York NY

JUDY CHICAGO Awarded in 1999
Virginia Wolf (Test Plate for "The Dinner Party"), 1978
Glazed porcelain, 14 in. diameter.
On loan from the National Museum of Women in the Arts,
Gift of Elizabeth A. Sackler in honor of Wilhelmina Cole Holladay

CLAIRE FALKENSTEIN   Awarded in 1981
Nid, 1958
Copper, 16.5 x 17 x 26 in.
©The Falkenstein Foundation
Courtesy of Michael Rosenfeld Gallery

SUE FULLER   Awarded in 1986
String Construction #70, 1956
String construction over board in wood and steel box, 36.25 x 48.25 x 1.5 in.
Courtesy of Michael Rosenfeld Gallery LLC, New York NY

NANCY GRAVES   Awarded in 1993
Frisson of Fear, 1995
Bronze, 48.25 x 27 14 x 30.5 in.
Courtesy of American University Museum

NANCY GROSSMAN   Awarded in 2008
Black Landscape, 1964
Leather, fabric, metal, wood, fur, bristle,
paper, nylon, and paint assemblage mounted to plywood, 49.875 x 38 x 3.5 in.
Courtesy of Michael Rosenfeld Gallery LLC, New York NY

GRACE HARTIGAN   Awarded in 1987
Spanish Thanksgiving, 1961
Oil on canvas, 56.75 x 53.13 in.
Courtesy of American University Museum

GRACE HARTIGAN Awarded in 1987
Trick or Treat, 1965
Oil on canvas, 72.25 x 60.125 in.
Courtesy of Michael Rosenfeld Gallery LLC, New York NY

MAREN HASSINGER   Awarded in 2009
Love, 2009
Pink plastic bags, dimensions vary
Courtesy of the Reginald F. Lewis Museum

LOÏS MAILOU JONES Awarded in 1986
Two Women, 1950
Oil on linen, 16.25 x 21 in.
Courtesy of Michael Rosenfeld Gallery LLC, New York NY

JOYCE KOZLOFF Awarded in 2009
If I Were a Botanist (Gaza), 2015
Mixed media on canvas, 54 x 91.25 in.
Courtesy of DC Moore Gallery

LEE KRASNER Awarded in 1980
Water No. 2, 1968
Gouache on Douglas Howell paper, 18 x 22 in.
Courtesy of Michael Rosenfeld Gallery LLC, New York NY

SAMELLA SANDERS LEWIS Awarded in 1989
White House, 1969
Oil on canvas, 36 x 30 in.
Courtesy of Dr. Diane Whitfield Locke and John Woo

EVANGELINE J. MONTGOMERY Awarded in 1999
In Memory of Martin, n.d.
Mixed media print, 47.5 x 43.5 in.
Courtesy of James E. Lewis Museum, Morgan State University

BEVERLY PEPPER Awarded in 1994
Untitled, 1980
Welded steel objects, 35.5 x 13.875 x 11.875 in.
Courtesy of Michael Rosenfeld Gallery LLC, New York NY

FAITH RINGGOLD   Awarded in 1994
The Sunflower Quilting Bee at Arles, 1995
Lithograph, 22 x 30 in.
Published as benefit print for CAA by the Brodsky Center, Courtesy of Judith K. Brodsky
BETYE SAAR Awarded in 1989
Blue Moon Neptune, 1989
Mixed media assemblage, 17 x 12 x 1.5 in.
Courtesy of Michael Rosenfeld Gallery LLC, New York NY

MIRIAM SCHAPIRO Awarded in 1988
In the Land of Oo-Bla-Dee, 1993
Mixed media silk screen print, 22 x 30 in.
Published as benefit print for CAA by the Brodsky Center, Courtesy of Judith K. Brodsky

JOYCE SCOTT   Awarded 2010
Pretty Girl Veiled, 2012
Nigerian wood object, plastic and glass beads, thread, and fabric, 44 x 24 x 26 in.
Courtesy of Goya Contemporary Baltimore

JOYCE J. SCOTT Awarded 2010
Soul Erased-Want a Little Action, 2000
Lithograph, 30 x 22 in.
Courtesy of Goya Contemporary Baltimore

ELIZABETH TALFORD SCOTT   Awarded in 1987
Voyage to the Bottom of the See, 1992
Fabric, thread, ricks, beads, buttons, shells, 69 x 57 in.
Private Collection

SYLVIA SLEIGH   Awarded in 2011
Paul Rosano, Seated Nude, 1973
Oil on canvas, 56 x 42 in.
On loan from the National Museum of Women in the Arts
Gift of Mr. and Mrs. Russell Bowman

NANCY SPERO   Awarded in 2003
Lovers, 1963
Oil on canvas, 55 ½ x 80 1/2 in.
Courtesy of Michael Rosenfeld Gallery LLC, New York NY

LENORE TAWNEY   Awarded in 1983
A Million Golden Birds, 1967
Mixed media collage of printed and cut papers with feathers, 6.875 x 10.125 x .5 in.
Courtesy of Michael Rosenfeld Gallery LLC, New York NY

CHARMION VON WEIGAND   Awarded in 1982
the Paradise Gambit, 1964-65
Oil on canvas, 45 x 40 in.
Courtesy of Michael Rosenfeld Gallery LLC, New York NY

RUTH WEISBERG   Awarded in 2009
The Blessing, n.d.
Oil, mixed media on canvas, 80 x 96 in.
Courtesy of Jack Rutberg Fine Arts

CLAIRE ZEISLER Awarded in 1982
Untitled, c. 1975
Colored and natural fiber construction with painted metal base, 49.25 x 24.5 x 10 in
Courtesy of Michael Rosenfeld Gallery LLC, New York NY

ALSO ON DISPLAY:

Slideshow of all 194 Women's Caucus for Art Lifetime Achievement Honorees

Select Lifetime Achievement Award catalogs

Posters from the WCA conferences in Washington, DC in 1979 and 1991.

Selected publications by the following Lifetime Achievement honorees:
Adeline Breeskin, Mary D. Garrard, Whitney Chadwick, Judy Chicago, Wanda Corn, Joanna Frueh, Suzi Gablik, Eleanor Gadon, Thalia Gouma-Peterson, The Guerilla Girls, Ann Sutherland Harris, Leslie King-Hammond, Samella Sanders Lewis, Suzanne Lacy, Lucy Lippard, Eleanor Munro, Ellen H. Johnson, Margo Machida, Joan Marter, Amalia Mesa-Baines, Linda Nochlin, Arlene Raven, Charlotte Streifer Rubinstein, Lowry S. Sims, Gloria Steinem, Marilyn Stokstad

Issues of *Heresies* to which many honorees contributed.

Issues of Woman's Art Journal edited by honorees Elsa Honig Fine (1980- 2006) and Joan Marter, including articles on many of the WCA Lifetime Achievement Award honorees.

LIFETIME ACHIEVEMENT AWARD HONOREES

Bernice Abbott	1982	New York
Bella Abzug	1980	Washington DC alternate awards
Mary Adams	1994	New York
Joyce Aiken	2001	Chicago
Anni Albers	1980	New Orleans
Emma Amos	2004	Seattle
Edna Andrade	1983	Philadelphia
Eleanor Antin	2006	Boston
Ida Applebroog	2008	Dallas
Tomie Arai	2016	Washington DC
Ruth Asawa	1993	Seattle
Helène Aylon	2016	Washington DC
Judy Baca	1998	Los Angeles
Jo Baer	2004	Seattle
Tritobia Hayes Benjamin	2010	Chicago
Vera Berdich	1992	Chicago
Ruth Bernhard	1981	San Francisco
Theresa Bernstein	1991	Washington DC
Camille Billops	2002	Philadelphia
Ilse Bing	1990	New York
Bernice Bing	1996	Boston
Isabel Bishop	1979	Washington DC
Nell Blaine	1986	New York
Betty Blayton-Taylor	2005	Atlanta
Louise Bourgeois	1980	New Orleans
Phyllis Bramson	2014	Chicago
Adelyn Breeskin	1981	San Francisco
Judith K. Brodsky	2002	Philadelphia
Beverly Buchanan	2011	New York
Selma Burke	1979	Washington DC
Diane Burko	2011	New York
Linda Frye Burnham	1999	Los Angeles
Margaret Taylor Burroughs	1988	Houston
Leonora Carrington	1986	New York
Rosalynn Carter	2005	Atlanta
Elizabeth Catlett	1981	San Francisco
Whitney Chadwick	2012	Los Angeles
Barbara Chase-Riboud	2007	New York
Judy Chicago	1999	Los Angeles
Minna Citron	1984/1985	Los Angeles/Toronto
Irene Clark	1995	San Antonio

Jacqueline Clipsham	1995	San Antonio
Sue Coe	2015	New York
Alessandra Comini	1995	San Antonio
Clyde Connell	1984/1985	Los Angeles/Toronto
Mildred Constantine	1991	Washington DC
Wanda Corn	2007	New York
Margret Craver	1989	San Francisco
Sheila Levrant de Bretteville	2016	Washington DC
Dorothy Dehner	1983	Philadelphia
Eleanor Dickinson	2003	New York
Sari Dienes	1981	San Francisco
Elsie Driggs	1982	New York
Tina Dunkley	2013	New York
Carolyn Durieux	1980	New Orleans
Maria Enriquez de Allen	1994	New York
Marisol Escobar	2006	Boston
Claire Falkenstein	1981	San Francisco
Alicia Craig Faxon	1996	Boston
Elsa Honig Fine	1996	Boston
Joanna Frueh	2008	Dallas
Sue Fuller	1986	New York
Suzi Gablik	2003	New York
Elinor Gadon	2006	Boston
Ofelia Garcia	2011	New York
Mary D. Garrard	2005	Atlanta
Paula Gerard	1992	Chicago
Dorothy Gillespie	2001	Chicago
Grace Glueck	2003	New York
Shifra M. Goldman	1993	Seattle
Thalia Gouma-Peterson	2001	Chicago
Nancy Graves	1993	Seattle
Nancy Grossman	2008	Dallas
Juana Guzman	2016	Washington DC
Harmony Hammond	2014	Chicago
Jo Hanson	1997	Philadelphia
Ann Sutherland Harris	2005	Atlanta
Ronne Hartfield	2003	New York
Grace Hartigan	1987	Boston
Maren Hassinger	2009	Los Angeles
Ester Hernandez	2009	Los Angeles
Wilhelmina Holladay	2001	Chicago
Elizabeth Gilmore Holt	1982	New York
Dorothy Hood	1988	Houston
Michi Itami	2004	Seattle

Mary Jane Jacob	2010	Chicago
Lotte Jacobi	1983	Philadelphia
Buffie Johnson	2007	New York
Ellen Johnson	1983	Philadelphia
Sonia Johnson	1980	Washington DC alternate awards
Marie Johnson-Calloway	2001	Chicago
Loïs Mailou Jones	1986	New York
Sister Theresa Kane	1980	Washington DC alternate awards
Leslie King-Hammond	2008	Dallas
Gwen Knight	1993	Seattle
Ida Kohlmeyer	1980	New Orleans
Joyce Kozloff	2009	Los Angeles
Stella Kramrisch	1983	Philadelphia
Lee Krasner	1980	New Orleans
Sadie Krauss Kriebel	1997	Philadelphia
Katharine Kuh	1982	New York
Yayoi Kusama	2006	Boston
Suzanne Lacy	2012	Los Angeles
Jean Lacy	1995	San Antonio
Artis Lane	2013	New York
Ellen Lanyon	2001	Chicago
Elizabeth Layton	1990	New York
Clare Leighton	1989	San Francisco
Susana Torruella Leval	2013	New York
Helen Levitt	2004	Seattle
Lucy Lewis	1992	Chicago
Samella Sanders Lewis	1989	San Francisco
Lucy R. Lippard	2007	New York
Otellie Loloma	1991	Washington DC
Yolanda Lopez	2008	Dallas
Helen Lundeberg	1981	San Francisco
Margo Machida	2009	Los Angeles
Muriel Magenta	2002	Philadelphia
Joan Marter	2011	New York
Agnes Martin	2005	Atlanta
Agueda Salazar Martinez	1993	Seattle
Amalia Mesa-Bains	1995	San Antonio
Dorothy Miller	1986	New York
Trinh T. Minh-ha	2012	Los Angeles
Agnes Mongan	1987	Boston
Evangeline J. Montgomery	1999	Los Angeles
Barbara Morgan	1986	New York
Maud Morgan	1987	Boston
Celia Alvarez Muñoz	1995	San Antonio

Eleanor Munro	2003	New York
Elizabeth Murray	2007	New York
Alice Neel	1979	Washington DC
Senga Nengudi	2010	Chicago
Louise Nevelson	1979	Washington DC
Linda Nochlin	2002	Philadelphia
Louise Noun	1992	Chicago
Georgia O'Keeffe	1979	Washington DC
Mine Okubo	1991	Washington DC
Ferris Olin	2012	Los Angeles
Yoko Ono	2005	Atlanta
Grace Paley	1980	Washington DC alternate awards
Rosa Parks	1980	Washington DC alternate awards
Beverly Pepper	1994	New York
Delilah Pierce	1991	Washington DC
Howardena Pindell	1996	Boston
Marianna Pineda	1996	Boston
Adrian Piper	2014	Chicago
Yvonne Rainer	2004	Seattle
Arlene Raven	1999	Los Angeles
Eleanor Raymond	1984/1985	Los Angeles/Toronto
Faith Ringgold	1994	New York
Rachel Rosenthal	1994	New York
Moira Roth	1997	Philadelphia
Charlotte Streifer Rubinstein	1994	New York
Betye Saar	1989	San Francisco
Miriam Schapiro	1988	Houston
Carolee Schneemann	2011	New York
Elizabeth Talford Scott	1987	Boston
Joyce J. Scott	2010	Chicago
Kay Sekimachi	1997	Philadelphia
Joan Semmel	2013	New York
Helen Serger	1990	New York
Bernarda Bryson Shahn	1989	San Francisco
Honoré Sharrer	1987	Boston
Lowery Stokes Sims	2008	Dallas
Sylvia Sleigh	2011	New York
Barbara T. Smith	1999	Los Angeles
Kiki Smith	2015	New York
Jaune Quick-to-See Smith	1997	Philadelphia
Nancy Spero	2003	New York
Spiderwoman Theater	2010	Chicago
Edith Standen	1988	Houston
Bernice Steinbaum	2012	Los Angeles

Gloria Steinem	1980	Washington DC alternate awards
May Stevens	1990	New York
Marilyn J. Stokstad	2002	Philadelphia
Margaret Tafoya	1992	Chicago
Anna Tate	1992	Chicago
LenoreTawney	1983	Philadelphia
Jane Teller	1988	Houston
Joyce Treiman	1984/1985	Los Angeles/Toronto
Pablita Velarde	1990	New York
Charmion von Wiegand	1982	New York
Ruth Waddy	2001	Chicago
Emily Waheneka	1993	Seattle
Kay WalkingStick	1996	Boston
Pecolia Warner	1983	Philadelphia
June Wayne	1984/1985 Los	Angeles/Toronto
Ruth Weisberg	2009	Los Angeles
Faith Wilding	2014	Chicago
Martha Wilson	2015	New York
Rachel Wischnitzer	1984/1985	Los Angeles/Toronto
Beatrice Wood	1987	Boston
Claire Zeisler	1982	New York

WCA PRESIDENTS

2014-2016	Brenda Oelbaum, Artist, Ann Arbor, MI
2012-2014	Priscilla Otani, Artist and Director of ARC Gallery, San Francisco, CA
2010-2012	Janice Nesser-Chu, Artist and Educator, St. Louis, MO
2008-2010	Marilyn J. Hayes, Artist, Arlington, VA
2006-2008	Jennifer Colby, PhD, Lecturer, San Juan Bautista, CA
2004-2006	Dena Muller, Executive Director of ArtTable and A.I.R. Gallery, New York, NY
2002-2004	Noreen Dean Dresser, Artist, New York, NY
2000-2002	Magi Amma, Sculptor and Activist, Santa Cruz, CA
1999	Gail Tremblay, Artist and Educator, Olympia, WA
1998	Transition Leadership Committee: Magi Amma, Catherine Carilli, Margaret Lutze, Gail Tremblay
1996-1998	Imna Arroyo, Educator, Eastern Connecticut State University, Wilimantic, CT
1994-1996	Helen Klebesadel, Artist and Educator, Madison, WI
1992-1994	Jean Towgood, Artist, Huntington Beach, CA
1990-1992	Iona Deering, Artist, Dallas,TX
1990	Carol Heifetz Neiman, Artist, Los Angeles, CA
1988-1990	Christine Havice, Associate Professor, University of Kentucky, Lexington, KY
1986-1988	Annie Shaver-Crandell, Associate Professor of Art History, City College of New York, NY
1984-1986	Ofelia Garcia, President, Rosemont College, Rosemont, PA
1982-1984	Muriel Magenta, Professor of Art, Arizona State University, Tempe, AZ
1980-1982	Susan DeRenne Coerr, Artist and Registrar, Fine Arts Museum of San Francisco, CA
1978-1980	Lee Ann Miller, Dean, Cooper Union School of Art, New York, NY
1976-1978	Judith K. Brodsky, Associate Provost Rutgers, State Univ. of New Jersey, Newark, NJ
1974-1976	Mary D. Garrard, Professor of Art History, The American University, Washington, DC
1972-1974	Ann Sutherland Harris, Professor of Art History, University of Pittsburgh, PA

The occupation or positions listed reflect those at the time of the presidency.

SELECTED BIBLIOGRAPHY

Arai, Tomie, and Lydia Yee. *Tomie Arai: Double Happiness*. Bronx, New York: Bronx Museum of the Arts, 1998.

Aylon, Helene. *Whatever is Contained Must be Released: My Jewish Orthodox Girlhood, My Life as a Feminist Artist*. New York: The Feminist Press at CUNY, 2012.

Benjamin, Tritobia H. *The Life and Art of Loïs Mailou Jones*. San Francisco: Pomegranate Artbooks, 1994.

Benjamin, Tritobia H. and Leslie King-Hammond. *Three Generations of African-American Women Sculptors: A Study in Paradox*. Philadelphia: Afro-American Museum of History and Culture, 1996.

Breeskin, Adelyn Dohme. *Mary Cassatt: A Catalogue Raisonné of the Graphic Work*. Washington, DC: Smithsonian Institution Press, 1979.

Broude, Norma, and Mary D. Garrard. *The Expanding Discourse: Feminism And Art History*. New York: Westview Press, 1992.

_____. *Feminism and Art History*. New York: Harper & Row, 1982.

_____. *The Power of Feminist Art: The American Movement of the 1970's History and Impact*. New York: Harry N. Abrams, 1996

Burnham, Lynda Frye and Steven Durland. *The Citizen Artist: 20 Years of Art in the Public Arena: An Anthology from High Performance Magazine* 1978-1998. Jenkintown, PA: Critical Press Inc., 1998.

Chadwick, Whitney. *Women, Art, and Society*. New York: Thames and Hudson, 1990.

Chadwick, Whitney, and Dawn Ades. *Mirror Images: Women, Surrealism, and Self-Representation*. Cambridge, MA: MIT Press, 1998.

Chadwick, Whitney, and Isabelle De Courtivron. *Significant Others: Creativity & Intimate Partnership*. New York: Thames and Hudson, 1993.

Chicago, Judy. *Through the Flower: My Struggle as a Woman Artist*. Garden City, N.Y. : Doubleday, 1975.

_____. *The Dinner Party: A Symbol of our Heritage*. Garden City, NY: Anchor Press/Doubleday, 1979.

Constantine, Mildred and Jack Lenor Larsen. *Beyond Craft: Art Fabric*. New York:Van Nostrand Reinhold Company; 1973

Corn, Wanda M. *The Great American Thing: Modern Art and National Identity, 1915-1935*. Berkeley: University of California Press, 1999.

_____. *Women Building History: Public art at the 1893 Columbian Exposition*. Berkeley: University of California Press, 2011

Faxton, Alicia Craig. *Dante Gabriel Rossetti*. New York: Abbeville Press, 1989.

Fine, Elsa Honig. *The Afro-American Artist: A Search for Identity.* New York: Holt, Rinehart and Winston, 1973.

——. *Women & Art: A History of Women Painters and Sculptors from the Renaissance to the 20th Century.* Montclair, NJ: Allanheld & Schram/Prior, 1978.

Frueh, Joanna. *Erotic Faculties.* Berkeley: University of California Press, 1996.

——. *Monster/Beauty: Building the Body of Love.* Berkeley: University of California Press, 2001.

Frueh, Joanna, Cassandra L Langer, and Arlene Raven. *New Feminist Criticism: Art, Identity, Action.* New York: Icon Editions, 1994.

Gablik, Suzi *Has Modernism Failed?* New York: Thames and Hudson, 1984.

——.. *Progress in Art.* New York: Rizzoli, 1977.

——. *The Reenchantment of Art.* New York,: Thames and Hudson, 1991.

Gadon, Elinor W. *The Once and Future Goddess.* New York: Harper One, 1989

Garrard, Mary D. *Artemisia Gentileschi around 1622: The Shaping and Reshaping of an Artistic Identity.* Berkeley: University of California Press, 2001.

——. *Artemisia Gentileschi: The Image of the Female Hero in Italian Baroque Art.* Princeton: Princeton University Press, 1989.

——. *Brunelleschi's Egg: Nature, Art, and Gender in Renaissance Italy.* Berkeley: University of California Press, 2010.

Gedeon, Lucinda H., with Michael Brenson and Lowery Stokes Sims. *Elizabeth Catlett Sculpture: A Fifty-Year Retrospective.* Seattle: University of Washington Press, 1998.

Glueck, Grace. *New York: The Painted City.* Salt Lake City: Peregrine Smith Books, 1992.

Glueck, Grace, and Paul Gardner. Brooklyn: People and Places, Past and Present. New York: H.N. Abrams, 1991.

Goldman, Shifra M. *Contemporary Mexican Painting in a Time of Change.* Austin: University of Texas Press, 1981.

——. *Dimensions of the Americas: Art and Social Change in Latin America and the United States.* Chicago: University of Chicago Press, 1994.

Goldman, Shifra M, Charlene Villaseñor Black, and Chon A Noriega. *Tradition and Transformation: Chicana/o Art from the 1970s through the 1990s.* Los Angeles: UCLA Chicano Studies Research Center Press, 2015.

Gouma-Peterson, Thalia. *Anna Komnene and Her Times.* New York: Garland Publishing, 2000.

_____. *Miriam Schapiro: A Retrospective, 1953-1980.* Wooster, OH: College of Wooster, 1980.
_____. *Miriam Schapiro: Shaping the Fragments of Art and Life.* New York: Harry N. Abrams Publishers, 1999.

Gouma-Peterson and Marion E. Jackson. *Ruth Weisberg: Paintings, Drawings, Prints, 1968-1988.* New York: Feminist Press at CUNY, 1988.

Guerrilla Girls. *Bitches, Bimbos, and Ballbreakers: The Guerrilla Girls' Illustrated Guide to Female Stereotypes.* New York: Penguin Books, 2003.

—— *The Guerrilla Girls' Bedside Companion to the History of Western Art.* New York: Penguin, 1998.

Hammond, Harmony. *Lesbian Art in America: A Contemporary History.* New York; Rizzoli, 2000

Harris, Ann Sutherland and Linda Nochlin. *Women Artists: 1550-1950.* Los Angeles: Los Angeles County Museum of Art, 1976.

Hartfield, Ronne. *Another Way Home: The Tangled Roots of Race in One Chicago Family.* Chicago: University of Chicago Press, 2004.

_____. *Musings on Barbarous Beauty: A Conservation Series on Art and the Sacred.* Cambridge, MA: Center for the Study of World Religions, Harvard Divinity School, 2004.

Holt, Elizabeth Gilmore *Documentary History of Art, 3 vols.* Princeton: Princeton University Press, 1949, 1958, 1966.

Jacob, Mary Jane, *Michael Brenson, and Eva M. Olson. Culture in Action: A Public Art Program of Sculpture* Chicago. Bay Press, 1995.

Johnson, Ellen H. *American Artists on Art from 1940 to 1980.* New York: Harper & Row, 1982.

_____. *Modern Art and the Object: A Century of Changing Attitudes.* London:Thames & Hudson, 1976

King-Hammond, Leslie. *Gumbo Ya Ya: Anthology of Contemporary African-American Women Artists.* New York: Midmarch Arts Press, 1995.

_____. *Ashes to Amen: African Americans and Biblical Imagery.* New York: Museum of Biblical Art, 2013.

King-Hammond, Leslie and Betye Saar. *Betye Saar: Colored : Consider the Rainbow.* New York: Michael Rosenfeld Gallery, 2002.

King-Hammond, Leslie and Lowery Stokes Sims. *Art as a Verb: The Evolving Continuum: Installations, Performances and Videos by 13 African-American Artists: November 21, 1988 - January 8, 1989.* Baltimore, MD: Maryland Institute, College of Art, 1989.

Kuh, Katharine. *My Love Affair with Modern Art: Behind the Scenes with a Legendary Curator.* New York: Arcade Publishing, 2012.

La Moy, William T. and Joseph P McCaffrey. *The Journals of Grace Hartigan,* 1951-1955. Syracuse, NY: Syracuse University Press, 2009

Leval, Susanna Torruella. *Voice from our Communities: Perspectives on a Decade of Collecting at El Museo del Barrio.*

New York: El Museo del Barrio, 2001.

Lewis, Samella Sanders. *African American Art and Artists*. Berkeley: University of California Press, 2003.

Lewis, Samella S., Richard J Powell, and Jeanne Zeidler. *Elizabeth Catlett: Works on Paper, 1944-1992*. Hampton, VA: Hampton University Museum, 1993.

Lewis, Samella S, and Ruth G Waddy. *Black Artists on Art*. Los Angeles: Contemporary Crafts Publishers, 1969.

Lippard, Lucy R. *Eva Hesse*. New York: New York University Press, 1976.

——. *From the Center: Feminist Essays on Women's Art*. New York: Dutton, 1976.

——. *The Pink Glass Swan: Selected Essays on Feminist Art*. New York: New Press, 1995.

Machida, Margo. *Unsettled Visions: Contemporary Asian American Artists and the Social Imaginary*. Durham, NC: Duke University Press, 2008.

Marter, Joan M. *Dorothy Dehner: Sixty Years of Art*. Katonah, NY: Katonah Gallery, 1993

Miller, Dorothy. *The Life and Work of David G. Blythe*. Pittsburgh, PA: University of Pittsburgh Press, 1950.

Minh-Ha, Trinh. *Woman, Native, Other. Writing Postcoloniality and Feminism*. Bloomington: Indiana University Press, 1989.

——. *D-Passage: The Digital Way*. Durham NC: Duke University Press, 2013.
——. *When the Moon Waxes Red: Representation, Gender, and Cultural Politics*. New York: Routledge, 1991..

Mongan, Agnes and Paul J. Sachs. *Drawings in the Fogg Museum of Art, 2 vols*. Cambridge: Harvard University Press, 1946.
Munroe, Alexandra, Yoko Ono. *Yes Yoko Ono*. New York: Japan Society, H.N. Abrams, 2000.

Munro, Eleanor C. *Originals: American Women Artists*. New York: Simon and Schuster, 1979.

——. *The Encyclopedia of Art: Painting, Sculpture, Architecture, and Ornament from Prehistoric Times to the Twentieth Century*. New York: Golden Press, 1961.

Miller, Dorothy. *12 Americans*. New York: Distributed by Simon and Schuster, 1956.

_____. *Americans 1963*. Garden City, NY: Distributed by Doubleday, 1963.

Miller, Dorothy Canning and William S. Lieberman. T*he New Japanese Painting and Sculpture: An Exhibition*. Garden City, NY: Doubleday, 1966.

Nochlin, Linda. *Representing Women*. New York: Thames and Hudson, 1999.

——. *Women, Art, and Power and Other Essays*. New York: Harper & Row, 1988.

_____. *Patterns of Desire: Watercolors by Joyce Kozloff.* New York: Hudson Hills Press : 1987.

Okubo, Mine *Citizen 13660.* Brooklyn: AMS Press Inc, 1966.

Pindell, Howardena. *The Heart of the Question: The Writings and Paintings of Howardena Pindell.* NewYork: Midmarch Arts Press, 1997.

Piper, Adrian. *Out of Order, Out of Sight.* Cambridge, MA: MIT Press, 1996.

Raven, Arlene. *Crossing Over: Feminism and Art of Social Concern.* Ann Arbor, MI: UMI Research Press, 1988.

_____ *June Wayne: A Retrospective.* Purchase, NY: Neuberger Museum of Art, 1997.

_____. *Nancy Grossman.* Brookville, NY: Long Island University, 1991.

Raven, Arlene, Cassandra L Langer, and Joanna Frueh. *Feminist Art Criticism: An Anthology.* Ann Arbor, MI: UMI Research Press, 1988..

Ringgold, Faith. *We Flew Over the Bridge: The Memoirs of Faith Ringgold.* Durham, NC: Duke University Press, 2005.

Roth, Moira. *Rachel Rosenthal.* Baltimore: Johns Hopkins University Press, 1997.

Rubinstein, Charlotte Streifer *American Women Artists: From Early Indian Times To The Present.* New York: G.K. Hall, 1982.

Schapiro, Miriam. *Miriam Schapiro: Works on Paper: A Thirty Year Retrospective.* Tucson, AZ: Tucson Museum of Art, 1999.

Schneemann, Carolee. *Carolee Schneemann: Imaging Her Erotics: Essays, Interviews, Projects.* Cambridge, MA: MIT Press, 2002.

Schneemann, Carolee, and Bruce R McPherson. *More than Meat Joy: Complete Performance Works & Selected Writings.* New Paltz, NY: Documentext, 1979.

Scott, Joyce and George Ciscle. *Joyce J. Scott Kickin' It with the Old Masters.* Baltimore: Baltimore Museum of Art, 2000.

Sims, Lowery Stokes. *Challenge of the Modern: African-American Artists 1925-1945.* New York: Studio Museum in Harlem, 2003.

Sims, Lowery Stokes and Leslie King-Hammond. *The Global Africa Project. New York*; Munich: Museum of Arts and Design; Prestel, 2010.

Standen, Edith Appleton. *Women Artists: The Metropolitan Museum of Art Miniatures.* Book of the Month Club, 1956.

Steinem, Gloria. *Outrageous Acts and Everyday Rebellions* 1983

Stokstad, Marilyn. *Santiago de Compostela in the Age of the Great Pilgrimages.* Norman, OK: University of Oklahoma Press, 1978.

Stokstad, Marilyn. *Art History, 2 vols. 1st ed*. New York: Prentice-Hall, 1995

Tawney, Lenore Tawney and Sigrid Weltge-Wortmann. *Celebrating Five Decades of Work*. Browngrotta Arts, 2000

Von Wiegand, Charmion. *Charmion von Wiegand: Retrospective*. London: Annely Juda Fine Art, 1974.

Von Wiegand, Charmion. *Charmion von Wiegand: Spirituality in Abstraction, 1945-1969*. New York: Michael Rosenfeld Gallery, 2000.

Waddy, Ruth G. *African-American Artists of Los Angeles: Ruth G. Waddy*. Los Angeles: University of California, Los Angeles, 1993.

Weisberg, Ruth, Robert Barrett, and Mac McCloud. *Ruth Weisberg Prints: Mid-Life Catalogue Raisonné, 1961-1990*. Fresno, CA: Fresno Art Museum, 1990.

Wischnitzer, Rachel. *Synagogue architecture in the United States: History and Interpretation* Jewish Publication Society, 1955.

Zeisler, Claire. *Claire Zeisler*. New York: Hadler Galleries, 1976.

Prepared by Aiden Faust, Leslie King-Hammond, Helen Langa, and Barbara Wolanin.

THANK YOU
to all those who contributed to IMPACT!

American University Museum staff:
Director and Curator Jack Rasmussen, Assistant Director Kristi-Anne Caisse, Lucy Crowley, Kevin Runyon, Bruce Wick, and all of their team

Curator Leslie King-Hammond

Lenders and donors:
American University Museum
Helène Aylon
Judith K. Brodsky
Diane Burko
DC Moore Gallery, New York NY
Goya Contemporary, Baltimore MD
Giselle Huberman
HIRO
Jack Rutberg Fine Arts , Los Angeles CA
James E. Lewis Museum, Morgan State University, Baltimore MD
Michael Rosenfeld Gallery LLC, New York NY
with special thanks to Halley K. Harrisburg
National Museum of Women in the Arts, Washington DC
Private Collections
Reginald F. Lewis Museum, Baltimore MD
Joyce J. Scott
Dr. Diane Whitfield Locke and John Woo
WCA National Board Members

to all who provided advice, assistance, support, and time:

American University Art History Department
Professor Emerita Mary Garrard
Professor Helen Langa
Graduate Students Annika Collins, Jenna Michael, and Skyler Simoneaux

Women's Caucus for Art
President Brenda Oelbaum
Past Presidents Marilyn Hayes and Janice Nesser-Chu
Co-Organizers Jaimianne Amicucci and Barbara Wolanin
Designers Jaimianne Amicucci and Amanda Rogers
WCA/DC Chapter Members Sonia Friedman, Stephanie Pickens, and Mary Jo Tydlacka
WCA Friends Jane Hill and Aiden Faust